Brian's Flying Book

By Brian Lansburgh

For more information, or to contact the author, visit
www.TailwheelersJournal.com.

© 2013 Brian Lansburgh. All Rights Reserved.

ISBN 978-1-304-10379-6

My thanks –

I had a lot of help putting this book together.

Many thanks to Mike Bowman for the wonderful words of the forward.

Special thanks to Jami Engebretson for her expertise in editing and publishing.

My proofreading team of Pat Anderson, Carolyn Stull and Gayle Crowder really helped keep me from looking like an idiot.

Bert Garrison not only provided many of the photos used in this book, but has been a wise counselor as well.

Mike Dennis gave me some sound advice and may possibly be blamed for this thing being published as soon as it is!

Kirby ("Mister Enthusiasm") Mills has been a constant encouraging influence as I try to follow my course.

And thanks to all of the enthusiastic readers and subscribers to the Tailwheeler's Journal and all those tailwheel students who have helped convince me that what I have to say just might be worth saying.

Brian Lansburgh

Dedicated to the memory of my first aerobatic coach, Tom Jones, "Famous Airshow Pilot".

Tommy, you will keep on swoopin' in the minds of all those whose lives you touched and influenced.

*Mark,
all my best wishes
for "Happy Swooping"!

Bill*

Introduction by Mike Bowman

Mike Bowman served in the Navy as a Naval Aviator for more than 35 years. He has flown over 5000 flight hours in 40 aircraft types and completed 1274 day and night carrier landings. During his career he flew more than 250 combat missions in Vietnam and Desert Storm. Mike has commanded a Light Attack Squadron, three Carrier Air Wings, a Carrier Strike Group and the Naval Aviation Training Command. His final tour was as Commander Naval Air Force Pacific in charge of all Pacific based aircraft carriers and U.S. Navy squadrons.

After my family, aviation is my second love in life. My Dad soloed me on my sixteenth birthday. Following college I entered Naval Aviation flight training and was lucky enough to have access to a cockpit throughout the 35 years I was fortunate to serve. Somewhere in there I developed, like many pilots, military or civilian, the opinion that I had learned pretty much all there was to know about flying. After all, what could be more challenging than bringing a single seat, light-attack jet (read very little rudder required) aboard a carrier at night? Then I met Mr. Lansburgh.

For my 50th birthday, as a surprise present, my wife enrolled me in Brian's Stick and Rudder Master Class. That was twenty years ago but I remember it as if it were yesterday. I met him for our first flight at a small strip east of Jacksonville, Florida. Shortly after takeoff Brian was introducing me to the joys, and challenges, of precision balanced, but more importantly, **unbalanced** flight maneuvers. Early on in that first flight I rediscovered that those pedals down there really do have a use for something other than braking the aircraft on the ground. I was immediately impressed with not only his flying skills, but also how extremely effective he was as an instructor. About mid-way through the course (which I was frankly hoping would never end) I asked Brian if he would consider teaching our son, Geoff, to fly. Initially he hesitated as it would require him to regain CFI currency, but as our friendship grew and my pressure continued he finally relented.

Our son's foundation in aviation is very strong as a result. Brian's course of instruction included pretty much everything you will read here. On the day of his solo I beamed as I watched him doing side slips, one-wheel landings out of a turning approach and many other maneuvers that were so impressive to see being flown by a pilot with only a few hours. It was clear he had a good coach. Geoff went on to enter Naval Aviation training shortly thereafter. He flies the FA-18 today. Whenever, as it often does, the subject of flying comes up between us, he thanks me for allowing him to learn the basics from Brian.

Brian Lansburgh is a truly talented pilot who has, more than anyone I know, dedicated his life to aviation. We remain fast friends to this day and I am so proud to be endorsing his fine book. Between the covers is an extraordinarily complete dialogue from which every pilot, regardless of experience, skill level or type of fixed wing aircraft, can benefit. His writing ability matches his superb oral instructional skills. The various maneuvers are laid out in a straightforward, easily understood manner with a line of humor thrown in from time to time. Any pilot who takes the time to read this fine publication and then go up and **practice, practice, practice**, will find themselves a far better and much safer pilot for it.

I know you will enjoy the read. Fly safe and fly often.

Happy Swooping.

Mike

Mike Bowman, VADM, USN (ret.)

Table of Contents

WHO NEEDS TO LEARN THIS STUFF?	19
PREPARING TO LEARN	19
CHECKLISTS	20
HOW AM I GOING TO ORGANIZE ALL THIS STUFF?	20
HAND PROPPING	21
THE TAILWHEEL: WHAT A GREAT INVENTION!	27
THE AVIATION BRAKING SNOBBISM PHENOMENON	28
FLYING THE BLIND TAILDRAGGER	30
TWO BASIC TAKEOFFS	31
THE CROSSWIND TAKEOFF	32
THE SAFE DEPARTURE	33
THE IMPORTANCE OF COORDINATION	36
THE ACCELEROMETER: THE RODNEY DANGERFIELD OF INSTRUMENTS	39
THE MANEUVERS	42
ADVERSE YAW DEMO	43
QUICK TURNS	43
THE DUTCH ROLL	44
STALLS	45
SKY DOODLING	47
ALTERNATING SIDE SLIPS	48
THE WHOOPEE STALL	50
LAZY EIGHTS	51
SPINS	53
ON-COURSE DESCENDING SLIPS	54

ARE YOU WORKING TOO HARD?	58
THE EXPOSUROMETER: EVERY PILOT SHOULD HAVE ONE	58
ENGINE FAILURE (GULP!)	60
INBOUND	61
WATER SKIING	61
THE PATTERN	63
A WORD ABOUT MANNERS	67
THE ABBREVIATED APPROACH	70
THE RADIO	70
THE STRAIGHT- IN APPROACH	74
LANDINGS	75
THE ESSENCE OF THE TAILWHEEL AIRPLANE	75
KEEPING IT STRAIGHT	77
COURSE AND HEADING	77
THE HIGH SPEED FLARE	78
THE THREE-POINT LANDING	78
THE CURSE AND BLESSING OF TAILWHEEL STEERING	81
THE WHEEL LANDING	82
ANATOMY OF A BOUNCED LANDING	84
PLANTING THE WHEELS	84
THREE-POINT VS WHEEL LANDING	85
WIND GRADIENT AND THE CROSSWIND LANDING	86
TOUCH AND GO OR FULL STOP?	87
INTRO TO ONE-WHEEL WORK	88
LANDING IN A TURN	89

UP ON ONE-WHEEL	92
THE SLALOM	92
THE DUTCH TOUCH	95
THE ONE-FOOTED TAKEOFF	95
THE 360 DEGREE OVERHEAD APPROACH	97
THE GO-AROUND	100
"DON'T MAKE STEEP TURNS CLOSE TO THE GROUND!"	102
FLAPS, POWER AND A WORD ABOUT ACCURACY	103
THE SHORT FIELD LANDING	105
FLIGHT IN FORMATION	109
A PARTING WORD	119

FORWARD

I suppose everyone who writes a book on flying looks in his library and compares what he has to say to what others have said before. I did, and that may be why my book is so skinny. Other writers have done a wonderful job of explaining much about the art and science of flying airplanes. I don't think there's much point in my repeating what writers like Langewiesche, Buck, Kershner, Schiff and others have already done so well. My area of expertise is in the largely uncharted realm of precision performance flying and the disappearing specialty of flying tailwheel airplanes. For the most part I'll try to stick to it. I have found that over the years I teach far more tailwheel courses than master classes. For that reason I'm now providing this master class book to all my tailwheel students. Not only does it contain descriptions of all the maneuvers I teach in a tailwheel course, but it also features some of the more advanced maneuvers from the Master Class. My Tailwheel Endorsement Course is six hours. Any pilot who finishes the course in less time will be introduced to advanced maneuvers in the time remaining.

Some very bad people were responsible for getting me into this mess. I was heavily influenced in my early career by Bill Warren, a gifted teacher and air show pilot, who demonstrated the fun side of flying and high performance precision flying close to and touching the ground (and water). I have long blamed Bill for getting me into the air show business. Bill taught flying until the day he died.

Like many pilots, some of my earliest work was flight instruction. I was trained as a CFI primarily by George DeMartini in the late seventies. George was a very serious, monklike zealot who preached the importance of pure taildraggy, instruments-covered attitude flying fundamentals. He hasn't changed.

With a brand new instructor certificate in my pocket I went to work for Terry and Jean Weathers at Montague Aviation in Northern California. I will always be grateful to the Weathers' for giving me my first shot at teaching and for introducing me to sailplanes. Though inexperienced, I tried to bring some originality to the job and constantly explored less conventional means to improve the quality of my instruction. In those early days of my instruction career I assumed that every established technique needed changing or improvement. That attitude cost me my job because I used to tape the stall warner on the wing of the school 152. It was a practice Terry did not approve of. He was broad-minded, though, and fired me not because I taped the stall warner, but because I always forgot to un-tape it. I learned a lot from Terry. I learned that most conventional flight instruction techniques are well founded and make sense. I also learned that the primary student sometimes needs certain hard indicators, like airspeeds and power settings, to hang his hat on in the early stages of instruction. My current radicalism is only aimed at areas where I feel that conventional flight instruction has failed to teach, cheated the student or planted dangerous misconceptions. And I still tape stall warners.

The late Al Heuston was a major influence on me when I was at Montague. Al was a strong-willed character who taught me a lot about stick and rudder work and turned me loose to check myself out in his Pawnee and Stearman. He also taught me a lot about life. I've never forgotten his trust.

A lifelong love of the entertainment business called me into air show flying where I found a niche doing a comedy act. Because my area of specialization was comedy flying, I became adept at very unusual attitudes and maneuvers. After an air show, local pilots would often express great interest in these maneuvers. The flat turn was particularly fascinating to most pilots who'd never tried it. It was while giving a little impromptu instruction to a few such pilots that I discovered how practice of some of those unusual maneuvers could really improve the ability of the average flier. I began to develop a syllabus for a course of instruction based on what I'd learned in the air show business. That course has evolved from something like "Brian Shares Secrets of Comedy Stunt Pilots", to the "Stick and Rudder Master Class". What you are reading started out as a textbook to accompany the course. But since it seems to have elicited such intense response, both positive and negative, I thought, "Why not just let these thoughts stand on their own as my book on flying". So here it is. Bearing in mind that this book started out as the handout accompanying my course, please remember this warning, often found on old fashioned restroom towel machines: "WARNING: PLACING YOUR HEAD IN TOWEL LOOP MAY RESULT IN INJURY OR DEATH!" When flying airplanes, putting your head somewhere else can cause injury or death so please keep your head out of that place and remember that this book has limitations. There's no reason it can't help someone who will never take dual from me. But remember that some of the maneuvers taught in the course could be extremely hazardous unless practiced under the supervision of a flight instructor who is familiar with the concepts of my course. There are very few such instructors.

I've found that much of my instruction is remedial in nature and wouldn't be necessary if the student had been taught correctly in the first place. If you are a student pilot or someone who is about to start learning to fly, I understand your position. When you're a neophyte it's next to impossible to judge competent instruction from its more common counterpart. My advice is to stay away from the low-time CFI who is instructing just to build time. And stay away from the high-time CFI who teaches on autopilot. Find yourself someone with a lot of experience who loves to fly and loves to teach. Come to think of it, there aren't many of those either! If you are a more experienced pilot looking to perfect your skills, try to find the same type of instructor who can actually do some of these maneuvers himself. I suggest starting with instructors who have air show flying experience. Some of the maneuvers described in this book can be practiced without an instructor on board. If you have any doubts about which are which, just email me at brian@tailwheelersjournal.com. I will always be available to offer an opinion.

My version of the towel dispenser warning is this: If you plan to try the more advanced of these maneuvers in your plane without any qualified instruction, please tell your survivors now that the coming crash will not be my fault.

I believe that a huge percentage of successful air show pilots are self taught. However, virtually all of them will advise that you get qualified aerobatic instruction. It's sort of a "Do as I say, not as I do" attitude. Patty Wagstaff once watched me practicing acro in my Cub before an air show.

"Are you self-taught?", she asked me.

"Why, yes", I replied.

"Well, in that case, you're not too bad", she observed.

I think there was a lot of wisdom in Patty's observation. Although a course of instruction is always the best way to go, it's often not the way we learn in the real world. If you can get instruction, do it. Otherwise, practice and proceed conservatively. You're certainly not going to kill yourself by simply tightening up your landing accuracy.

I believe that if more pilots could handle their aircraft with the skills I've always tried to teach, we'd have fewer wrecks. I also feel that modern pilots reach a certain level of proficiency and then stop seeking to improve. I'll give you an example: Most pilots aim for the airport and are satisfied to land somewhere near the centerline. How come they don't pick an exact spot and try to land there on every landing? The key is a desire to improve and the willingness to practice. My goal is to help pilots who were previously limited to herding their planes around the sky to become airmen in the true sense of the word, at home in the air and truly skilled at controlling their aircraft with precision.

Finally, you may not agree with some of my theories. That's fine. One guy read an early draft of this little book and called me to raise hell over my section on radio usage. He had a different opinion. I don't know why he got so worked up, but he was wasting his time. If you don't agree with me, don't adopt my practices. I don't think I'm going to change many pilots. Those yayhoos will still be flying five miles away to enter on a forty-five and they'll still be burning up the airwaves with unnecessary calls, regardless of what I think and whether or not they read this little book. I've had fun writing it. I hope you'll have fun reading it and perhaps putting some of my ideas to use. Oh, and some of my best friends are "yayhoos".

I have been accused of having a pretty snobbish attitude regarding the skill level of the average general aviation pilot. Guilty as charged. The average pilot can't fly as well as a day-old dodo. Flying ability is the product of training, practice and talent. Many pilots have lots of talent. Very few have had good training and even fewer practice sufficiently to become more skillful.

This intro is going to be longer than the book if we don't get on with it. Let's go flying.

Brian Lansburgh

Sisters, Oregon, 2013

WHO NEEDS TO LEARN THIS STUFF?

Some pilots are surprised to learn how much "bad training" baggage they are carrying around. Most don't know they have any. Remember how dumb you felt when you first started learning to fly? For one thing, you had no way to tell how good a particular instructor was because you just had no knowledge base with which to judge him. And no matter how smart a guy[1] you are, you may still be carrying around a few bad habits learned in good faith. Here's a test. Ask yourself these questions:

Was the stall warner ever disabled during your training? Were the airspeed indicator and the turn coordinator ever covered? Did you get much spin training? Did you practice flight at minimum controllable airspeed? (They call it "slow flight" now. The first name is more appropriate). Were you taught intentional cross-controlled or uncoordinated flight other than during landings? Will you ever consider a turn back to the runway if the engine fails on takeoff? Should you ever make a steep turn close to the ground? Do you know what two conditions must exist for most light singles to spin?

If you answered "no" to any of these questions, you could probably use a little review of your piloting techniques and maybe the practice of some of the maneuvers that are described in this book. If you answered "no" to all the questions, you desperately need to reconsider a lot of the things you were taught and presently assume about flying.

PREPARING TO LEARN

Of all the reading you can do, my strongest recommendation is for Wolfgang Langeweische's book entitled, appropriately enough, "Stick and Rudder". It's the best book I've found on the art and science of flying. It's a shame that it hasn't been more widely utilized as a textbook by students and instructors. There are actually flight instructors who've never heard of it! If you

---

[1] I refuse to use terms like "he or she". All my personal pronouns are masculine and you're supposed to know that women are always included.

haven't read it before, I'm sure you will enjoy it and gain valuable insights from it, regardless of your level of experience. Langewiesche compares an airplane to a horse, which has "gaits". This makes perfect sense to me and I familiarize all my students with the airplane's main gaits of "normal climb", "normal cruise" and "normal glide", as well as the very important "cruise descent".

CHECKLISTS

My favorite pre-takeoff acronymic checklist is "CIFFTRRS", pronounced "Sifters". It stands for: Controls, Instruments, Flaps Fuel, Trim, Run-up, Radio and Seatbelts. Remember, if you use such a checklist, you've got to think about all the items under one heading. For example, "Fuel" also includes the fuel selector, fuel quantity, fuel boost pump, mixture, etc. Even more pilots like to use "CIGAR TIP": Controls, free and moving properly; Instruments ; Gas, both quantity and set on correct tank, alternate fuel pump on or off as appropriate: Altimeter: Run-up; Trim set for takeoff; Interior, doors and windows locked; Propeller set for takeoff.

Most people use the pre-landing checklist, "GUMPS". It stands for: Gas, Undercarriage, Mixture, Prop, Seatbelts.

At shutdown I'm fond of "Mixture, Master, Mags", although not necessarily in that order. You'll want to turn radios off before shutdown and if you turn off the master before pulling the mixture you will protect your radios from voltage spikes.

The feds insist on the use of written checklists during checkrides. 'Nuff said.

HOW AM I GOING TO ORGANIZE ALL THIS STUFF?

We're going to structure this book as we would a flight. We'll takeoff, perform some maneuvers, enter the pattern and work on our landings. Since I've combined the Master Class and the Tailwheel Course, we'll leave the trikes in the hangar. We're flying a tailwheel airplane and the section on takeoffs will have little meaning for someone flying a tricycle gear aircraft. On the other hand, the three-point landing technique is just as appropriate for a tricycle gear airplane as it is for a taildragger. But before we can go anywhere, we've gotta figure out how to start this thing.

HAND PROPPING

There are a few things we teach in a tailwheel course that have nothing to do with the tailwheel itself. That's because so many tailwheel airplanes are older. Many older airplanes exhibit more adverse yaw than more modern airplanes. That's why we concentrate on coordination skills. Many older airplanes lack starters and that's just one reason why we really should include a section on hand propping. My Cub didn't have a starter and the L2 that I taught in for years didn't have a starter. Lately I've been adding hand propping to the syllabus for many of my tailwheel endorsement applicants even though my Cessna 140 is equipped with a starter. **If you don't remember anything else from this section, remember this: If you never get in the arc of a propeller, you will never get hit by a propeller.**

Luckily, tailwheel airplanes are more suitable for hand propping because their tail-low attitude puts the prop higher and easier to pull through. A tricycle gear airplane can be propped but you'll find yourself bending down during the pull through and it's more difficult to get your energy moving away from the prop during the process.

It's my opinion that hand propping is comparable to "popping the clutch" to start your car. Every driver should know how to start his car with the clutch if the starter goes out. Every pilot should know how to hand prop his airplane if it's proppable. If you fly an airplane that is capable of being hand propped and you don't know how to do it, you should go home. Come back with some old geezer who can teach you how to prop it.

Hand propping is a pretty simple operation. But, because of the inherent dangers if improperly done, it's a good idea to learn proper technique. It's also good to understand some additional engine basics.

Impulse Couplings

Many engines are equipped with an "impulse coupling". This little doohickey gives one or both of the magnetos a brief acceleration in order to produce a hot spark for starting. The impulse coupling consists of flyweights and spring assemblies which connect the magneto to the accessory shaft. When the crankshaft is turned at low speed (when turned by hand or even by a starter) the magneto is temporarily held while a spring is compressed until the pistons reach approximately top dead center. At this point the magneto is released. It then quickly rotates as the spring kicks back to its original position. Because it's turning fast for a moment, the magneto produces a hot spark. Once the engine is running and the magneto has reached a speed at which it furnishes sufficient current, centrifugal force causes the flyweights in the coupling to fly outward and lock the mag to the accessory gear. The magneto is now in a normal timing position relative to the engine. You can tell if a magneto is equipped with an impulse coupling by the sharp clicking noise it makes as the crankshaft is turned slowly. You can tell which magneto has the coupling by noting from which mag the click comes. This is important because the impulse coupling not only produces hotter spark but it also changes the timing on that mag. It retards that spark so that it occurs closer to top dead center. This decreases the chance of advanced spark causing either kick back or slower rotation. For this reason, we often start engines equipped with one impulse mag by selecting only that mag for starting. We then select "both" once the engine starts. The presence of an impulse coupling can make it possible for us to hand prop an engine.

Priming

A cold engine generally will need to be primed with fuel before it will start. That's the purpose of primer pumps. But personally, I like to prime small Continentals with the prop. I think it distributes the fuel better. All that's required to perform this priming is to make sure the throttle is closed, the mags are off or grounded and that the aircraft is secured with tiedown and chocks. Then you simply pull the prop through in the normal direction of rotation several times. Usually you can hear the carb "slurping" fuel as you pull it through. In addition to this pulling through, you can also pump the engine by rocking the prop a couple of times on each cylinder's compression stroke. A fully primed intake system will often be indicated by some dripping of fuel from the carb. Coincidently, that dripping can also help start an induction fire (fuel good; fire bad). My Cub used to catch fire all the time. I'd just stick my face down there and blow it out. People witnessing that routine would often gasp or just shuffle away, shaking their heads.

Here's a great idea from the Geezer Patrol[2]: Turn the fuel selector off right before propping the engine. That way, should anything go wrong, the engine won't run for very long. However, it will run long enough for you to get from the front of the airplane to the cockpit in order to turn it back on if everything is under control.

Securing of Aircraft

It's usually considered safer to have a qualified person in the pilot's seat while you prop the plane. That person can apply the brakes and operate the mag switch and throttle, making the process much more efficient. However, I'd rather do it all by myself than have someone who doesn't know what they are doing occupying the pilot's seat.

---

[2] *The Geezer Patrol is that ubiquitous group of seniors who can be found at almost any airport. They are often retired from flying but not from volunteering advice and help. They are our valuable connection to the past. Some of them have driven me nuts on occasion, but I love 'em. Treat them with respect; someday you will join their ranks if you live long enough.*

Most people agree that having the airplane well secured is a sound prerequisite for hand propping if you don't have someone in the pilot seat. I agree, although it makes a huge difference whether you're propping from in front or behind the prop. Cubs and other tandem aircraft can be propped from behind and, honestly, if there is no one to help AND the plane is not tied down or chocked you can get away with propping it successfully.... most of the time. But the only time I think I could honestly justify propping an unsecured airplane was the time I'd landed at the closed airport at Rajneeshpuram and a truckload of enraged Rajneeshees were bearing down on me. Not only did I prop my Cub without regard to securing the airplane, but I also took off without bothering to put on my seatbelt. After all, the truck was getting really close! Oh, I also propped it unsecured during my airshow comedy act... but that was showbiz!

Propping an L2 from behind. He'll raise the blade, adjust his fingers and bring it swiftly down.

So, if you don't have armed zealots bearing down on you with unknown but suspicious intent and you're not in showbiz, take the time to secure the airplane. The minimum is to tie the tail. Tying both tail and wings are even better. There are scads of instances where airplanes that were hand propped got away from their pilots and did incredible damage. Take the time to secure. The consequences aren't worth doing otherwise.

Fundamentals of Technique and Dispelling Geezer Crap

When it comes to the actual technique of hand propping, there are really only three factors to consider. You want to make sure that no part of your body is directed into the arc of the propeller while you are flipping it through, you want to be able to get a reasonable number of blades pulled through in a minimum amount of time since it may take several blades before the engine starts and you don't want the plane to leave without you.

There are two places to stand while propping: In front of the plane or behind the propeller on the right side of the nose (for American planes). Most tandem seated planes like the J-3 Cub are best propped from behind. They are relatively narrow in the nose and there is room for you to stand beside the nose while you swing the prop through with your right hand (In fact it's the ONLY way you can prop a Cub on floats). Your left hand should be holding onto the plane at some point like the open door frame. This is a relatively bullet proof technique when it comes to safety. With that death grip on the plane, you shouldn't be able to inadvertently get smacked by the prop. And, from this position, you can get to the throttle or ignition in a heartbeat. Unfortunately, most airplanes are too wide to accommodate this position and we're forced to prop them from the front. If a hand propped airplane gets away from you while you are in front of it, you'll find it difficult or impossible to both get out of the way **and** to get to the controls as the aircraft lurches past you on the way to its date with destruction.

As in golf, first we must address the propeller. From the front of the airplane, rotate the prop so that as you face the plane, the prop is slanted at forty-five degrees. The upper blade will be just at the beginning of its compression stroke[3] and as you swing it down you should be completing that cycle just as you step away. The prop will be in the same position if you are behind it. The only difference is that you'll only be able to swing it with one hand instead of two.

---

[3] *Propellers are installed so that they are in this position at top dead center. If yours is not, it's been installed incorrectly. It's an easy thing to neglect if a starter is always used, but it can make hand propping difficult or impossible.*

The best way to ensure that you will not get smacked by the prop is to have the energy of your swing help move your body away from the prop as you pull it through. Interestingly, those who are most afraid of getting hit are the ones most likely to because they stand really far from the prop, then have to lean into it in order to swing it. That leaves them poised to fall right into the prop arc. Those who stand closest to the prop are then able to easily step away from it as they complete the prop swing.

When I was in the air show biz, I'd occasionally get volunteers eager to prop my Cub (I think there may be a little link between testosterone production and hand propping for some members of the Geezer Patrol). I almost always regretted it. In their zeal to show that they knew what they were doing, these guys would go through that strange routine where they spit on their hands, yell "contact" and "switch on" and all those other arcane terms and then grasp the upper blade and proceed to throw their right leg up like a drunken Nazi on parade. Then they'd kick that leg down and back as they pulled the prop down and through its cycle. If the engine started on that first, rather lengthy, try it would have been great. Of course it never did, so we had to witness the whole operation again (picture lots of eye-rolling on my part). That whole leg flinging routine is ridiculous and succeeds only in putting someone out of balance close to the prop. The whole routine takes so long that if the danged thing doesn't start on the first couple of tries you'll be there all day. Just stand reasonably close to the prop and give it a flip while stepping away.

As far as the communication between the propper and the guy at the controls, the main thing we're concerned about is brake, throttle and ignition. I've always liked to confirm with the occupant that we've got "brakes on, cold and closed". Before flipping the prop through, I'll grasp the prop and give it a push to confirm that the brakes are applied. "Cold and closed" refers to the ignition being off and the throttle being closed. When I'm satisfied that the engine is primed and ready to start, I'll call for "hot and brakes", confirming that the ignition is now on and the brakes are still applied (the stick should be back as well).

Where to Grasp the Prop

The propeller should be grasped half way between the tip and the hub. Any further out will give you better leverage but will make it difficult to pull the prop through with suitable rotational speed. If you can apply enough torque while grasping the blade closer to the hub you should do so.

The trailing edge of the prop's airfoil is the spot that your fingers will naturally want to curl around in order to have a good grasp. Be careful about wrapping your fingers around that trailing edge. If your fingers' first joints are on that edge and the prop kicks back it'll be painful. I like to use the friction of my fingers and hands on the face of the prop to provide the grip. I don't allow the trailing edge of the prop to contact my fingers any further in than halfway into the pads of my fingertips. That way if the prop kicks back as the result of advanced timing, it won't grab my fingers. We don't want this process to look like a Disney "How-To" cartoon featuring Goofy.

Hand propping is a skill that every pilot should have. Many people are afraid to attempt to hand prop. They shouldn't be. They simply need to understand how to do it properly. Propellers shouldn't be feared, just respected.

So we've got our little beater started and we're all strapped in and ready to go. On our way out to the runway, let's talk about some of the issues we'll need to deal with. Let's start with the device that lends its name to this course in the first place, the tailwheel.

THE TAILWHEEL: WHAT A GREAT INVENTION!

Back in the old days the early airplanes were configured much like our present tailwheel airplanes in that the center of gravity was behind the main gear. But the tail was supported by a skid when the plane was on the ground. Runways were nonexistent and the old planes were operated in big fields. They'd simply land and takeoff into the wind, their tailskids dragging on landing and takeoff. As aircraft became more sophisticated and started to be operated on runways it was an obvious improvement to replace that skid with a tailwheel. Then some smart guy invented brakes and another smart guy made the tailwheel swivel so that tight turns could be made on the ground. Another guy came along and hooked that swiveling wheel to the rudder so that rudder deflection also turned the tailwheel.

The Tailwheel... a thing of beauty on a cool, ski-equipped 170.

One of the final improvements was the addition of a mechanism that would allow the wheel to pop out of a detent, freeing it from the rudder interconnection if the side load was great enough. Now we had the best of all situations; nice interconnection to the rudder for positive steering of the tailwheel and the ability for it to pop out for really sharp turns when necessary. That is how most tailwheels operate now.

THE AVIATION BRAKING SNOBBISM PHENOMENON

One of the skills that sets the professional race car driver apart from us non-pros is his ability to determine the right amount of braking to use at the right time. Additionally, it would never occur to a professional driver to go out on the track with less than excellent brakes.

We pilots are taught to think differently about brakes. There exists a snobbism about brakes that has always fascinated me. Perhaps it's because the earliest airplanes had no brakes and pilots had to learn to plan ahead for landing rollouts and taxiing. To this day many pilots have a mindset against using brakes unless absolutely necessary and consider it a point of pride that their braking is so minimal.

I'm not one of those pilots. Just as the race car driver must be proficient in the use of brakes, I believe the pilot (and especially the taildragger pilot) must be similarly adept. You can't become adept without practice, so I say go ahead and brake all you want. Learn to use your brakes to make smooth short field landings. Learn to make those flashy rolling stops that terminate with a graceful 180 as the engine shuts down. Just observe these rules for proper braking: Don't try to make a tight turn from a standstill using one brake. Instead, get the plane rolling a little, and then smoothly apply power and brake to make the tight turn. Don't use power and both brakes at the same time while taxiing straight ahead; it's a waste of energy. The only exception is the stunt pilot tail-up taxi where power and brake are applied at the same time to keep the tail in the air at low speed or even at a stop. That's a maneuver I practice a lot. It is not without risk, so if you practice it, do it under the right conditions, with calm air or a steady headwind. Be very careful about depending on your brakes. Certain aircraft brakes are prone to catastrophic failure, especially when really needed. The Scott heel brake cylinders that are used in early Pipers and other planes are especially bad. These brakes don't use an actual cylinder. Instead they consist of a dome within which is mounted a round neoprene diaphragm. The circle of ten screws, which serve to secure the diaphragm between the dome and the pedal assembly, easily identifies these brakes. If the diaphragm is a little weak and you mash on the brake pedal it can rupture, leaving you with absolutely no brake on that side. If you have a plane equipped with those early Scott brake cylinders I highly recommend an STC'd conversion called a "brake booster". The dome and the diaphragm are removed and replaced with the booster assembly. It consists of a cylinder containing a piston with "O" rings. It will apply greater hydraulic pressure with the same amount of pedal pressure and there is no risk of catastrophic failure. There's a really great one made by Steve's Aircraft (www.stevesaircraft.com) and I think every old assembly should be upgraded with Steve's booster.

Greater use of brakes will up your maintenance costs somewhat because you'll have to re-line and re-disc more often, but I think the added proficiency is worth it. If I didn't, I wouldn't encourage my students to practice with the brakes that I pay for!

FLYING THE BLIND TAILDRAGGER

Although some taildraggers, like the Maule and the C-170, offer decent forward visibility over the nose, a lot don't. Steve Oliver, an air show pilot colleague and really smart airman, helped me define the discipline required to cope with the lack of visibility in these airplanes. Here's the secret:

You can't see over the nose, so don't try. While taxiing, weave back and forth. Look down the right side of the plane when you turn left and the left side when you turn right. Never try to look around the nose during a landing.

On short approach for a three-point landing you get your last good look at the runway. Take a mental snapshot of it. Then sit back, relax, depend on your peripheral vision for heading and altitude cues. Flare. DO NOT TRY TO LOOK AROUND THE COWLING DURING A LANDING! You won't see anything interesting and it will spoil your peripheral vision's point of view.

Steve isn't kidding when he says, "If you don't see the runway on your right and you don't see it on your left, it must be in front of you."

Most flights start with a takeoff, so let's get to it.

TWO BASIC TAKEOFFS

For the moment, let's disregard crosswinds, short fields, soft fields and obstacles at the end of the runway. That leaves us with two basic takeoff techniques, tail down and tail up.

Tail Down

We'll assume that the trim has been set for normal climb. In the tail down takeoff the aircraft's throttle is opened and it's kept on the center line with rudder as it accelerates. We apply no pressure to the elevator. As the aircraft accelerates, the horizontal stabilizer becomes effective and the aircraft assumes the normal climb angle of attack. Gradually its weight is transferred from its mains and tailwheel to its wings. It becomes lighter and lighter until it gradually leaves the ground and climbs. It's a perfectly acceptable technique in calm conditions, but it has a couple of drawbacks. One drawback is that, depending on the type of airplane, visibility over the nose is very limited until the tail comes up. The second drawback is that because the weight transfers from wheels to wings so gradually there is a tendency of the airplane to "hop" or "chirp" sideways on its mains as they gradually lose friction with the ground. If we keep the tail down even longer, this is a technique that I'd definitely prefer for a rough or soft field takeoff. We'd keep the tail inches off the ground until airborne, at which time we'd accelerate in ground effect before assuming the desired angle of attack for the climb out.

Tail Up

The second takeoff technique utilizes full forward stick as the throttle is opened. As soon as the elevator becomes at all effective the tail will begin to come up and weight will stay on the mains as the aircraft accelerates. Once the wings reach neutral angle of attack, we begin to relax the elevator in order to maintain that attitude. Once we achieve flying speed we smoothly but quickly increase the angle of attack to normal climb and the airplane leaves the ground. Here are the benefits to this technique: The weight of the plane is on the wheels until it is on the wings. There is much less tendency for the plane to hop and chirp while transitioning from one to the other. My friend Greg

Koontz, who is a very talented teacher and air show performer, claims that with the wings at zero angle of attack, the absence of induced drag will allow the plane to accelerate to flying speed using less runway, making this a good technique for short field takeoffs. Finally, if you're flying a "blind" airplane with its nose in the air you'll get your forward visibility much quicker.

"Don't Be 'Skeered!'"

I've found that many of my students are apprehensive about applying a bunch of forward stick. They fear that, without a nosewheel, the prop might impact the ground. It's really not an issue during a takeoff (it can become an issue during a landing rollout). As the tail comes up, the horizontal stabilizer goes from negative angle of attack to neutral angle of attack (Remember, it's an upside down airfoil). If the tail is forced higher than level, the relative wind will be pushing down on the stabilizer. As the plane accelerates, the downward force will increase. It will be nearly impossible for the elevator to overcome the horizontal stabilizer's downward push in order to put the plane's snoot into the ground.

While we're changing the pitch attitude of the plane on takeoff, it's a good idea to remember that the propeller is a large gyroscope. What happens when you move the axis of a gyroscope? Pressure applied at any point on the disc of a gyroscope is felt 90 degrees from that point in the direction of rotation. That means if we raise the tail of an airplane on takeoff, we are actually applying pressure forward at the top of the prop disc. That pressure will be felt 90 degrees in the direction of rotation, so the right side of the prop disc will tend to move forward, causing the airplane to yaw to the left. Aha! That's why the danged thing lurches to the left when I raise the tail on takeoff and explains why I have to apply right rudder at that time to avoid bouncing off the runway and into the puckerbrush!

THE CROSSWIND TAKEOFF

Most pilots are taught a crosswind takeoff technique that consists of putting in up-wind aileron before the airplane even starts to roll. Depending on the amount of crosswind, the airplane should be rolled up on that upwind wheel as it accelerates and stay on it until rotation. Most students disregard their early training in crosswind takeoffs and that can result in real problems later. A friend described an accident that occurred because the upwind wing was allowed to be raised by the crosswind. A Pawnee was destroyed as a result. This rise of the upwind wing should never be allowed. Let's review that original technique and reinforce it by practice: The takeoff roll is begun with full aileron into the wind. The aircraft is rolled up on the windward wheel as soon as there is sufficient roll authority. Aileron input is now decreased as necessary to hold the desired bank angle. Once on one-wheel the takeoff roll continues WITH THE WINDWARD WHEEL FIRMLY PLANTED. Upon reaching a relatively high rotation speed (see the section that refers to Greg Koontz' theory) my Pawnee is simultaneously rotated into the air and turned to its estimated crab heading with wings now level.

I have been practicing this takeoff, not to prevent the upwind wing from being caught by the crosswind, but simply to practice my own proficiency. To be honest, I went a long time without thinking about the dangers of crosswind takeoffs. By accident (and by exaggerating a takeoff maneuver commonly taught to primary students) I've been preventing such an event. It should be noted that this is another area where the tailwheel airplane has an advantage over its tricycle geared brother. A tailwheel airplane can assume an exaggerated wheel-planting pitch attitude on takeoff. A trike will scrub its nose wheel. The maneuver can be done in a trike, but not as effectively. A Pawnee is a low wing airplane so it can't assume as great a bank angle with one-wheel on the ground. The technique still works well in the low wing airplane but is even easier with the high winger.

THE SAFE DEPARTURE

All pilots are familiar with the way departures are taught at the modern Acme Flying Academy: Maintain runway heading until some certain altitude, usually about 800 feet. Make no turns until that altitude is reached. Even if the engine fails, land straight ahead rather than attempting anything but a slight (and shallowly banked) turn. I'm sorry, but this traditional technique drives me nuts.

I have maintained before that this is a procedure designed to protect under-trained pilots. Since our course is designed to increase piloting skill, let's look at ways we can increase the safety of the average departure by assuming that the pilot is properly trained and highly skilled.

First, we need to talk about airspeed. I'm convinced that most pilots climb out at a dangerously slow speed which gives them little time to assume a proper angle of attack in the event of engine failure. Do yourself a favor and accelerate in ground effect to something well over your airplane's published Vy (best rate of climb airspeed). That additional airspeed will give you time and distance to maneuver if the fan quits at low altitude. Climb at a lower rate in order to give yourself that insurance. Once you've got some altitude you can raise the nose to Vy in order to hasten your climb to cruising altitude. Vx (best angle of climb airspeed) is a dangerous option. If there is an obstacle to clear on takeoff it's usually best to aim for a lower part of it in order to gain speed and then zoom over it. The smart pilot is deciding whether to initiate that takeoff in the first place and all situations have to be analyzed, taking into account their own particular conditions.

Then, we have to change the way the average single engine pilot thinks about his exposure during departure. We can learn a lot from multi-engine procedures. The multi engine pilot is taught that the takeoff consists of stages. These stages determine at what point he can abort the takeoff, continue on one engine, land straight ahead or return to land on one engine.

Every takeoff for us should consist of stages and we should be calling them off to ourselves as we reach them. First comes the stage during which we can land straight ahead on the remaining runway. This is a wonderful option, but it doesn't usually last very long and we have to know when it runs out. Once we can no longer use the remaining runway we must decide where we're going to go. Let's assume for the time being that there are no other runways we can reach, that the runway we're departing on is the only runway and that no other suitable landing areas are reachable. There is a "dead man's zone" we must pass through. In that zone we don't have enough altitude to get back to the runway no matter how good our technique is. A straight ahead landing, even in horrible terrain is the only course of action. But once beyond the dead man's zone, we should try to plan for a return to the runway and take the actions necessary for that return even while the takeoff is proceeding normally. That's why I advocate the off-course departure, or turn after takeoff and here's why:

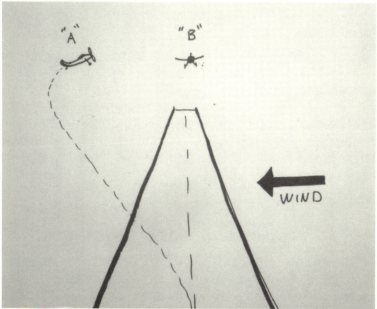

The pilot of airplane "A" has allowed the wind to blow him downwind of the extended centerline. The pilot of airplane "B" has crabbed to stay on the extended centerline. Both of their engines blow up at the same time. Pilot "A" will make it back. Pilot "B" will be smarter to land straight ahead in the briar patch... or boulder field.

Let's assume that the diameter of the tightest turn we can make is one hundred yards. If we reach an altitude from which we can lose an engine and still make a one hundred and eighty degree turn before reaching the ground, that turn will leave us one hundred yards to the side of the runway. But what if we changed course immediately after takeoff in order to reach a point one hundred yards to one side of the runway by the time we reached that critical turn-back altitude. Now if the engine should fail, we simply drop the nose, make a one-eighty and we're lined up on the runway. That's the basic theory of the off-course departure. Of course there are complicating factors that will always have to be taken into consideration and different airports, traffic and weather conditions will always require altering our planning to suit the circumstances. If there is a crosswind, the plane's off-course climb should be to the downwind side. That way you'll be turning into the wind if you have to return.

Of course there will always be the "Whuffos"[4], who challenge any technique other than the one taught in the modern Acme Flying School.

At Sunriver Soaring we were sometimes criticized for making downwind departures with the glider on tow. The moronic pedants who criticized this technique always assumed that we had our heads up our butts. It never occurred to them that in the event of a rope break or engine failure both the towplane and glider would be turning to make a landing into the wind, always a desirable technique. Radios and the MK 1 eyeball protected us from opposing landing traffic.

THE IMPORTANCE OF COORDINATION

We've got to climb up to an altitude to practice our coordination maneuvers and this is the perfect time to talk about the use of rudder in the climb. I won't get into a discussion of "P" Factor, Rotating Slipstream and Torque. I'll leave that to the Geezer Patrol to kick around in the airport bar. I will tell you that those effects will gang up on you to cause your airplane to yaw to the left in a climb. It's called "left turning tendency", but I think it should more rightly be called "left yawing tendency".

---

[4] A term borrowed from our skydiving brethren. A Whuffo is usually a stranger to aviation who asks, "Whuffo you jump outta them airplanes?"

If you sit on the extended centerline at the departure end of a busy runway you'll have lots of light single engine airplanes takeoff directly toward you and climb out over your head. I would guess that you will see at least 80 percent of these departing airplanes lower their right wings as they climb out. Their pilots are encountering left yawing tendency and are unconsciously banking to the right to correct it (They are also attempting to stay on the extended centerline, which could be a mistake, but we'll get into that later). This actually causes them to slip and degrades the climb performance of their airplanes. All they need to do to overcome this effect is to concentrate on keeping their wings level and then apply enough right rudder to stop any left turn. Period. That takes care of left yawing tendency.

Once airborne, it's time to test our coordination skills. This is an area where we can all use some improvement.

An extremely talented air show pilot and teacher, Bill Warren was often asked to teach aerobatics to other pilots. Bill told me that the number one problem he encountered when starting to fly with someone was that they were incapable of using aileron and rudder in a coordinated fashion. In fact, Bill would not teach aerobatics until the student was capable of good coordination. Bear in mind that these were not student pilots. They were all pilots who had sufficient experience that they felt comfortable in pursuing a course in aerobatics.

My experience has been the same as Bill's. My solution to the problem has been to teach not only coordination, but also controlled lack of coordination as a method for perfecting the pilot's proficiency in the use of rudder and aileron. Let's re-visit exactly what coordination is:

Remember that the primary purpose of rudder is simply to compensate for adverse yaw. Adverse yaw is the result of an increase in induced drag caused by the downward deflected aileron. When we turn, we simply have to depress enough rudder to keep the nose from yawing in the opposite direction of the bank. Fred Weick, who designed the Ercoupe[5], had that figured out and devised an interlock between rudder and aileron. His airplane didn't need rudder pedals to compensate for adverse yaw so you won't find rudder pedals on most Ercoupes. In my opinion, the Ercoupe is a tragic concession to under-training.

You can't do all the cool things like slips, hammerheads and slaloms down the runway unless you have rudder pedals, so a truly proficient pilot must, and should, master their use.

This is where the primary flight instructor is in a position to ingrain technique in a new student which will serve that student well for the rest of his flying days. Unfortunately, most modern, well-intentioned and otherwise competent instructors pass up this opportunity and instead do their students a disservice when they teach them that to coordinate a turn with proper use of rudder they should just look at the turn coordinator and "step on the ball". With that innocent sounding piece of advice the student has just been told to remove his attention from the outside of the aircraft (where it certainly belongs, especially in a turn) and re-focus it on an instrument. He is now supposed to ignore the cues his own body is giving him and stare at this little black ball for the same information. You see, that little black ball is nothing more than a weight suspended in space. It will stay in the center of the glass tube when the aircraft is in coordinated flight, but will slew toward the outside of the turn in a skid and the inside of the turn in a slip. In many ways the ball is a redundant instrument because it does the same thing that any unsecured weighted object will do under the same circumstances... the human body for example. If you will simply relax your upper body (don't lean into or away from your turns) you will be able to detect any skidding or slipping. When it comes to leaning, I think there are three types of people: Those who lean away from the direction of bank, those who lean into the bank and those who don't lean at all. The latter are the easiest to teach. If they find themselves leaning it's because of the effect of aerodynamics and they need only to apply enough rudder to center themselves in their seat. The others have to work a little harder at learning

---

[5] *Weick also designed the Pawnee, so we can forgive him for the Ercoupe (Watch those Ercoupe drivers come after me now!)*

to relax and use the appropriate amount of rudder.

It will take practice (I'm still working on it) and you may have to remind yourself to relax, but eventually you will develop a sense of coordination which will give that turn coordinator a real run for its money. And you won't be diverting your attention from the windshield where it belongs.

THE ACCELEROMETER: THE RODNEY DANGERFIELD OF INSTRUMENTS

Virtually all aerobatic aircraft are equipped with accelerometers or "G" meters. Almost no other aircraft are so equipped. Does this mean that only aerobatic pilots are influenced by the affects of acceleration? Of course not. In the Acme Flying School they've made airspeed the variable that's responsible for everything: Best glide (what the hell is that?), best rate of climb, best angle of climb, stalling speed straight and level, stalling speed with a steep bank, maneuvering speed, blah blah blah, it's always airspeed. Airspeed can only be judged with an indicator in the panel that may or may not be accurate[6]. "G" force, which is actually the main determinator of stall speed, is a force that can be felt by the body with no reference to instrumentation. My point is that if you have a "G" meter you can teach yourself to judge "G" force in a relatively short amount of time. Without it you have no idea and never will have. Every airplane I own has a "G" meter.

We were all taught at an early stage of our instruction that every airplane has a "maneuvering speed". In the event of turbulence, that's the speed we should fly in order to avoid tearing the ship apart. Why is that? "Because my flight instructor told me so"? No, the engineers who assigned that speed to your airplane knew that "maneuvering speed" was a

---

[6] I once saw a guy call the FBO for help because he had about ten miles to fly in order to get his rented 172 back to that FBO and the airspeed indicator didn't work. He was afraid to make a ten mile flight without an airspeed indicator. That's a sign of under training. Flying by reference to pitch is a perfectly safe way to fly and doesn't depend on instrumentation.

speed at which it was impossible to pull more than the maximum amount of "G" force that the airplane was capable of withstanding. They knew that '"G" available' was an important element, but did you ever hear the term '"G" available'? Probably not. I was a professional air show performer before I heard it. It was thanks to the efforts of two former Air Force pilots, Mike Van Wagenen and T.J. Brown, that these concepts were brought to a bunch of air show pilots who thought they were pretty hot sticks and who had never heard of '"G" available' or "corner velocity". "Corner velocity"? What's that? The corner velocity is simply the minimum speed at which an aircraft can pull its maximum rated "G"s. That's a pretty important speed, since a slower airplane turns tighter than a faster one, all other things being equal. An aircraft at corner velocity is capable of its best turn performance. Since I choose not to exceed three "G"s in most of the aircraft I fly, I need to find the minimum speed at which I can pull three "G"s. The size of the turn radius of an aircraft depends on the speed it is traveling. A faster aircraft requires a larger circle to turn in than a slower one. However, the turn radius isn't only a function of speed. It also depends on the number of "G"s a pilot pulls during the turn. An aircraft at a constant speed will make a relatively wide circle at 1.2 "G" but will turn in a very tight circle at 7 or 8 "G"s (if it's capable of pulling that many "G"s at that airspeed). The corner velocity is the speed that provides the best combination of turn rate and turn radius.

I've been fortunate to have spent some time experimenting with these concepts. After towing a glider to release altitude the tow pilot is faced with the goal of getting the towplane to the ground in the minimum amount of time but without cooling the engine too rapidly by too fast a power reduction or too high an airspeed. This means that the airspeed needs to be limited and the drag increased so that the airplane can descend rapidly without an increase in airspeed. How do we increase the drag? Naturally, flaps will help. The other way to increase drag is to load the aircraft with "G" force. We do this by rolling into a steep bank and hauling back. I found that the ideal combination in the PA25 Pawnee was about 90 miles an hour and three "G"s which results in about 1,500 to 2,000 feet per minute of descent. Without that "G" force such a rate of descent at that airspeed with power on is virtually impossible. With a couple of seasons of these descents after every tow, I had a lot of time to experiment with "G" force as a contributor to drag. Of course, after getting out of the plane, I did tend to stagger around in circles to the left and reply to every comment with "huh?" And my earlobes are now lower than they were a couple of years ago.

The accelerometer, or "G" meter". The center hand is the active hand, indicating that we are at about 1 "G". The other two hands are "tell-tales" and indicate the maximum negative and positive "G"s that we have experienced. In this case they show over 5 "G"s positive and about 1.5 negative. They can be re-zeroed by pushing the reset button.

Let's not ignore "G" force as one of the variables in our flight bag o' tricks. It's a force to be reckoned with when it comes to the practice of many of our maneuvers such as accelerated stalls, whoopee stalls and spin recoveries. It's also critical to our ability to rejoin a formation flight from the inside of a turn. You'll find out about that at the end of this little book.

Now that we've got coordination and "G" force all figured out, let's introduce some maneuvers which will hone that coordination as well as other piloting skills.

THE MANEUVERS

The following maneuvers, some of which are unique to the Stick and Rudder Master Class, are essential to the success of that course. These maneuvers all have something in common. They have been designed or selected because they give the pilot the opportunity to develop greater skill at a particular operation. They work because they use repetition (like the Portuguese Roll or Sky Doodling) or by drawing out or slowing down an operation (like the High Speed Flare). Most participants also find that these maneuvers offer a welcome challenge to their piloting skills.

Remember that a quest for precision is the key to improving your airmanship. Probably the greatest practitioner of precision high performance flying is Bob Hoover. Here's a quote from Bob. I found it in an old film. It indicates his humility as well as his respect for the risks of flying:

"I don't think I possess any skill that anyone else doesn't have. I've just had perhaps more of an opportunity--- and have been fortunate enough to survive a lot of situations that many others (didn't). ***It's not how close you get to the ground, but how precise can you fly the airplane?*** *If you feel so careless with your life that you want to be the world's lowest flying aviator, you might do it for a while, but then there are a great many former friends of mine who are no longer with us simply because they cut their margins too close."*

With Hoover's words ringing in our ears, let's start learning the maneuvers.

ADVERSE YAW DEMO

This is just about the first maneuver I do with every student of every level. If you are a primary student and your instructor hasn't demonstrated adverse yaw, fire him. Get another instructor. To demonstrate adverse yaw we put our feet on the floor and roll the airplane back and forth. We observe the phenomenon of adverse yaw that causes the nose to yaw opposite to the direction of bank. Once we know how much adverse yaw is present we put our feet back on the pedals and continue the rolls, compensating for adverse yaw. Preceding any coordination maneuvers with this simple demo seems to make it easier for us to feel how much rudder will be needed. Once we've got this under our belts it's logical to proceed with the next two maneuvers:

QUICK TURNS

This simple maneuver is just a series of level turns back and forth, each about thirty degrees either side of an average course. The amount of heading change is not important. The roll rate should be fast and the angle of bank anywhere between thirty and forty-five degrees. The purpose of this series of turns is to develop a sense of coordination while rolling in and out of bank and also to coordinate the use of elevator throughout the maneuver to maintain altitude.

This is an extremely important part of the training program. This is where we forget about that silly ball in the turn coordinator and start feeling our upper body. If we lean one way or the other as we bank it means we need more rudder on that side or maybe less of the wrong rudder we're applying. This is the basic method for determining coordination. If you've never practiced it you're in for a lot of time doing these maneuvers because it will take some time to develop the sensitivity. Believe me, it's worth it.

Remember the three kinds of people mentioned earlier? There are those who lean in the direction they are turning. They tend to be aggressive, but sometimes need to relax to feel coordination. There are those who lean away from every turn. I usually assume that they are a little apprehensive and are actually afraid of falling out of the airplane. They, too, need to learn to relax. With practice their confidence increases and they learn to coordinate. And then there are those who don't lean at all. They will learn coordination the soonest because they have no leaning baggage to check.

THE DUTCH ROLL

The Dutch Roll was the first maneuver Dwight Thomas taught me on my very first flying lesson. Some people are never taught this basic but important maneuver. It's an excellent basic coordination-building maneuver. I often use it to first evaluate a pilot's ability to coordinate rudder and aileron. The Dutch Roll consists of alternating rolls to a certain angle of bank (usually from twenty to forty-five degrees). The rolls are done briskly, with full aileron deflection (full deflection in a Cub, not a Pitts or F-18) the rolls alternate fast enough that, with proper use of rudder to compensate for adverse yaw, the aircraft's heading will never change.

Common errors are failure to match the amount of rudder to the amount of aileron, use of too steep a bank angle at first and timidity in the use of full aileron. Like most maneuvers, it's best to start small and work your way up to a greater degree of difficulty.

By the way, if you practice this maneuver while watching the ball, you may never get it right. In most airplanes, the ball swings in a more exaggerated fashion because it's so much lower than the wings (remember, the airplane IS the wing). I really think you're better off to ignore it and feel the coordination with your upper body, especially when rolling rapidly as you will in the Dutch Roll.

Speaking of Dutch Rolls, I met a young man in Florida many years ago. He hung out at the airport and I thought he had a lot of talent. I gave him some dual in my Cub. Months later I found out who he was. Without knowing it, I had given flight instruction to the stepson of Dwight Thomas, my first flight instructor. Tell me there's no Karma.

STALLS

I really don't care for the way we're expected to perform stalls according to the FAA (Remember, "Them what knows, does. Them what don't know, teaches. Them what don't know and can't teach, regulate"). I think that immediately recovering from a stall reinforces the misconception that they are dangerous or uncomfortable and keeps us from becoming familiar with that flight regime. I always start with the power on stall so that we're climbing as we practice. We'll simply raise the nose slowly while maintaining full power. We want to observe the pitch attitude when it "pays off" as well as how the stall breaks. Does it tend to drop a wing? Does it give us much warning? We want to see what it looks and feels like as it approaches that stalling angle of attack with full power. As the plane actually stalls, we will simply decrease the angle of attack. We will also observe the importance of rudder to maintain coordination as we perform our stalls.

Once comfortable with power-on stalls, we'll try them power-off. The Geezer Patrol really likes this method. Popularly referred to as the "Falling Leaf", this technique also eschews the standard recovery. Instead, we slowly increase the angle of attack, using rudder to keep from dropping a wing. We'll reach a point where the elevator is held all the way back. The airplane will start bobbing, searching for its flying speed. I usually lock the control wheel at this point (sometimes I forget to tell the student that I'm holding it and he panics, thinking that the stick has jammed... I gotta stop doing that!). I hold the elevator all the way back and neutralize the ailerons. The student then practices keeping the airplane in control with only rudder. We'll even practice some turns using only rudder. It's a fun, informative exercise.

With both types of stalls I stress that the angle of attack must be increased gradually to avoid an accelerated stall. No zooming, unless you want to turn this into a Whoopee Stall, which is described a little later.

I believe that the practice of certain maneuvers will help develop the right reflexes. Simulated engine failures at best angle of climb speed will help teach the importance of getting the nose down. Flight at minimum controllable airspeed helps develop reflexive rudder use to keep wings level. It also helps sharpen the ability to recognize the imminent stall. The Falling Leaf is a good maneuver as are cross-controlled stalls. Of the latter I like to run a student through three in a row as mentioned above. First the flat turning stall: A rudder is deflected fully while the wings are kept level with aileron. Then the angle of attack is increased until the stick is all the way back. Interestingly, in most light planes, the nose simply nods as dynamic stability causes the plane to search for speed. The outside wing's aileron usually maintains its roll authority. Then the forward slipping stall: The rudder is again fully deflected and sufficient opposite aileron held to keep the course constant. Then the stick is brought back gradually. Again, the airplane doesn't want to spin. Finally, the gently banked skidding turn: Imagining a situation where we've overshot the turn from base to final and are trying to increase the turn rate without banking steeply, we get ourselves into a shallow banked skidding turn. Then we pretend to attempt to both pull the nose up and stretch the glide by hauling back on the stick. Hold on to your hat 'cause the average Cub type taildragger will screw itself into a spin with little warning. Since most Acme-trained pilots use gradual power reduction during an approach, they may be carrying as much as 2,000 RPM as they perform that mind-numbing skidding turn. Since the power gives the elevator even more authority, the stall is snappier and the ensuing spin is really dramatic.

Bear in mind that the first two stalls were the ones which the uninitiated would suspect to be the most dangerous, but the last one is the one the undertrained pilot will most likely fall for.

I don't usually spend a lot of time on stalls unless I find that the student is afraid of them. In such a case I'll spend a little more time trying to correct that misplaced fear, replacing it with knowledge and competence.

My old pal, Zimmo, used to like to tell his skydiving students that "knowledge dispels fear". Or was it the other way around?

SKY DOODLING

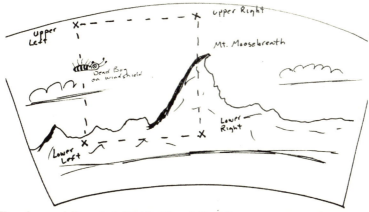

The view out the windshield: The dotted line represents where you'll put that dead bug as you perform the sky doodle, a square this time. It can be any shape.

Sky doodles are sometimes the first maneuver I use to help a pilot learn to isolate his hands and feet from each other. It also may be the maneuver which first illustrates the importance and difficulty of precision attitude flying. As with many maneuvers, we use the screw on the top of the cowling or a dead bug on the windshield as our pencil while we "draw" a figure on the horizon. We start with a square. Half of the square is above the horizon, half below. The square is not very big. If you extend your hand, fingertips up, it would just about cover the square. We start with the bug on the horizon (it's hard to get those bugs to commit suicide directly in front of our face where they belong). Then we raise the nose to draw the upper half of the left side of the square. Maintaining the resulting pitch attitude, we make a level turn to drag the bug to the right, drawing the top line. Rolling out and holding the resultant heading, we lower the nose to draw the entire right side vertical line. With the bug now below the horizon, we turn to the left to form the bottom line, stop, then pitch up to fill in the missing lower half of the left side and cover the previously scribed upper half of that line. We continue to repeat the process, drawing our square over and over. Pretty simple, huh? Now comes the next stage: We will repeat the maneuvers but we'll keep the wings absolutely level throughout the turns, climbs and descents. Now your turns are done with only rudder and every time you yaw with the rudder, you'll have to apply enough opposite aileron to prevent the plane from banking toward the applied rudder.

Once you get proficient at the square, we'll introduce the circle. It increases the degree of difficulty tremendously. By the time you can precisely draw the square and the circle, you've got a good handle on the skills necessary to perform subsequent cross-controlled maneuvers. You can practice these maneuvers while on a long cross-country flight without costing yourself much time. You should stop if your passengers start reaching for the barf bags.

ALTERNATING SIDE SLIPS

You could say that Alternating Sideslips and their cousins are the flagship maneuvers of the Stick and Rudder Master Class. It's a maneuver consisting of a series of alternating slips to equal and opposite angles of bank with the heading of the aircraft remaining constant at all times. I used to call this maneuver the "Portuguese Roll". I stopped when everyone tried to do it like a Dutch Roll.

We begin the maneuver from level flight at economy cruise. We could make altitude a constant, but normally I let it slide (It will automatically become a constant when we practice the ground reference variant). Noting a point on the horizon as our heading bug, we roll the plane to about 15 degrees of bank using coordinated rudder and aileron. When the airplane assumes its bank angle it will want to turn. Opposite rudder is smoothly fed in to prevent a heading change. This is a very dynamic maneuver because when you feed in that opposite rudder you will cause the airplane to want to bank in the direction of that rudder. So, you'll also find the need for an increase in the amount of opposite aileron, which will necessitate the need for more rudder. This tug of war between rudder and aileron will eventually cease when the aircraft is stabilized in its cross-controlled state with heading and bank constant. It is now in a sideslip. As soon as that equilibrium is reached, with no more need to increase either rudder or aileron, we roll the airplane to an equal and opposite angle of bank. This is a coordinated roll, using even more of the same rudder we are already holding. As soon as we reach the new bank angle we must smoothly change from coordinated to opposite rudder in order to maintain the heading. As soon as we once more attain equilibrium, we repeat the process.

The most common error is to forget that the rolls to the bank angles have to be coordinated. Instead, many pilots will depress opposite rudder as they initiate the roll. The result is to amplify the effects of adverse yaw, causing a wild heading excursion. Another mistake is to begin with a steep angle of bank. This makes the maneuver more difficult right from the start and slows the learning process. Remember, you learn faster when you start with smaller inputs and perfect the technique before increasing the difficulty.

This maneuver is difficult, not only because it's probably never been practiced before, but also because a lot of forces like adverse yaw and over-banking tendency gang up to make it hard. You simply have to watch the attitude of the aircraft and use stick and rudder to put it where you want it regardless of where it wants to be.

We'll use the same maneuver on low approaches to put the airplane alternately on each side of the centerline. During this variation it will require power and/or pitch changes to maintain a constant altitude close to the ground.

THE WHOOPEE STALL

Okay, now it's time to have a little fun and knock some of the rust off the "G" meter.

I stole this maneuver from the late Duane Cole, who described it in his aerobatic primer, "Roll Around a Point". I've modified the entry and recovery a little so that it's more like part of a full oscillation stall. Whatever you call it, I like it because it teaches a basic recovery technique that can be applied to other maneuvers, notably spins, and because it builds confidence in both the airplane's stability and the pilot's ability. Although it can be entered several ways resulting in varying severity, we'll standardize it as entered from level cruise. We'll bring the power back a couple of hundred RPM so it won't subsequently over speed. The nose is then lowered to a pitch angle of 45 degrees (Be careful that the increase in airspeed doesn't cause the RPM to increase to redline). Once entry airspeed (approximately 100 mph in the J-3) is reached the nose is briskly raised to 45 degrees of nose up pitch. Don't exceed 3 "G"s during this pull (one of the purposes of this maneuver is to learn what 3 "G"s feels like. You need to know this). Simultaneously the power is smoothly reduced to idle. Hold this pitch attitude! You'll have to continue to pull the stick back in order to maintain that attitude. Eventually the stick will be full aft, the stall will break and the nose will drop on its own. We keep the stick back while the plane, obeying its dynamic stability, searches for airspeed. Only when the aircraft's nose comes up on its own do we smoothly open the throttle, relax the backpressure a little and recover to a normal climb attitude. Obviously, once the ailerons quit being effective we depend on use of rudder to keep the nose straight and a wing from dipping.

Here are some common errors: Raising the nose too high results in a more whippy whoopee stall and one that's harder on the guy in the back seat (that would be me in a tandem airplane). Many pilots want to vigorously push the stick forward on recovery. If done early, that results in a high-speed dive with a subsequent high "G" pull; if done late, it results in an unnecessary altitude loss during recovery. The proper recovery consists of a slight relaxation of backpressure as the aircraft's own upward oscillation peaks, timed to coincide with the application of power. Many pilots fail to maintain wings-level throughout the maneuver, resulting in a change of heading and a tendency to drop off on one side at the break.

For many pilots, the Whoopee Stall will be their first experience with negative "G". As such, it's a pretty good maneuver to prepare for the forces and fun of aerobatics.

Oh, and here's an interesting fact with which non-aerobatic types may not be familiar: The steeper you dive, the less altitude you lose to reach your entry speed. Now **THAT** is an important tidbit of information.

LAZY EIGHTS

If you look in the FAA's Flight Training Handbook, you'll find a section on Lazy Eights. It will tell you how much pitch should be at about every forty-five degrees through the whole maneuver, along with how much bank at each heading and so on. If you try to hit all those reference points when you first start learning the maneuver you'll fry your brain (remember what I said about those who regulate). I like this maneuver, but I like to teach it with fewer reference points. I think that if you get comfortable with a simplified version, you'll learn it faster and can then start refining it. Remember that the Lazy Eight is simply an attitude flying maneuver where we "draw" a figure eight on its side, using our cartoon brush. Half of it is above the horizon and half below. You start at a specific heading and you complete 180 degrees of heading change before coming back. A lot of folks forget that you can use your wingtips to indicate 90 degrees of heading change. If you start with your nose on a landmark (I like mountain peaks in Central Oregon) and turn, your wingtip will be on that landmark when you've completed 90 degrees. Then, when you've completed another 90 degrees, your wingtip will be where your nose was at the previous 90 degree mark and your nose will be on a landmark that's 180 degrees from the starting landmark. I'm lucky because where I currently fly, I can get right between Mt. Moosebreath and Mt. Poophead, using them for my two main landmarks. Okay, so far, so good. We know the two landmarks that are 180 degrees apart and we know where the 90 degree mark is. Let's do it. Remember, this is one of those attitude flying maneuvers where it's best to pretend that we have a twenty-mile-long Walt Disney cartoon brush dripping with India ink. We're going to draw an infinity symbol or 8 on its side with half of the figure above the horizon and half of it below. What follows is a theoretical technique. We couldn't possibly do this legally, so this is all theoretical. Here we go: Starting with our nose on Mt. Moosebreath, we lower the nose to a nice entry speed, maybe 115 mph, with our engine RPM at about 2400 RPM (depending on the airplane). We won't touch the power again. We are going to draw a half circle above the horizon while in a right turn. Okay, we pull and draw that circle. Staying coordinated, we pull up, increasing our bank. I like to do these **theoretical Lazy 8's** at 90 degrees of bank by the time I reach the apex of the half circle (yeh, yeh, I know, it's only supposed to be 45 degrees, but this is more fun and why do you think we're here! If you are uncomfortable with 90 degrees of bank, stop. Get some dual. Fly with me, **theoretically speaking**.). That apex should be reached by the time we reach 45 degrees of turn, but don't worry about that right now. We're more concerned that the nose is coming back down through the horizon before it reaches 90 degrees of turn. As we pass through 90 degrees of heading change the lower half of the 8 is now executed while decreasing the bank so that the plane is going through wings level as our nose comes back up through the horizon right at Mt Poophead, which is at 180 degrees of heading change. The nose comes up through that 180 degree landmark while beginning its left bank which will increase to 90 degrees at the apex of that second above-the-horizon half circle. Don't forget your big ol' paint brush. You're slopping that India ink along a nice figure eight. Your nose will fall back through the horizon at the 90 degree point and you'll be rolling out of your bank as you start bringing the nose back up to intersect Mt Moosebreath right where you started. Wasn't that fun? The only parameters I care about when we start these eights is that I don't want to redline the engine, don't want to exceed 90 degrees of bank, don't want to exceed about 120 MPH (or a pre-determined speed depending on the aircraft) and, most importantly, don't want to exceed 3 "G"s. What, you don't have a "G" meter? Go home. And come back when you have one.

SPINS

One of my earliest students was an instructor's dream. He'd even taken my advice and bought a '46 Taylorcraft BC 12 D in which to learn to fly. In the course of his pre-solo instruction I spent a lot of time on spins. This guy could enter a spin and recover on a heading with the best of them. Most instructors would agree that his spin training was more than adequate. On his second solo flight he spun in, totaled the airplane and was fortunate to have crawled away from it alive. I did a lot of soul-searching after that. I didn't teach for two years. It really changed my approach to spin training.

Knowing how to spin and how to recover will not save you from the crash that results from an inadvertent spin at low altitude. From a safety standpoint it is far more important to recognize an imminent stall-spin than to know spin recovery techniques. The notable exception is the practice of aerobatics, in which case full familiarity with spin recovery techniques is imperative. I still teach spin entries and recoveries, but as proficiency maneuvers more than lifesaving ones. I now dedicate a lot of effort to teaching the awareness of conditions that can lead to the inadvertent spin. So in discussing spins we'll first deal with inadvertent ones and how to avoid them. Then, we'll get into spins as a challenging and fun proficiency maneuver.

I think that most people who study these things might agree that the spin entry which kills more people than any other is the one that starts when a pilot is trying to recover from an overshot turn from base to final. I think that, because so many pilots are afraid to steepen the bank in order to tighten that turn, they inadvertently skid that turn, trying to increase the rate of turn without increasing the bank. But that skid pulls their nose down, so they try to raise it while still skidding. "G" force increases, they reach stalling angle of attack and, because they are skidding, they spin. They are too close to the ground to recover. The result is tragically catastrophic. Remember, we talked about this situation in the section titled "Don't Make Steep Turns Close to the Ground". Because of this I include a series of three stalls in my course. The first is the forward slip stall, then the flat turn stall and finally, the skidding shallow banked stall. It surprises most of my students (most of whom are rated pilots) that it's the latter stall that most consistently whips them into an unexpected spin. This points out that, with very few exceptions, a coordinated airplane will not spin. A skidding airplane will spin if stalled.

When you learn to fly, you learn new habits and reflexes. Some come more quickly than others, some are good and some are harmful. Two of the most important reflexes you can develop are the reflex to get the nose down and the reflex to use rudder to keep a wing from dropping at high angle of attack. These reflexes are also evidently some of the hardest to develop. Before we learn how airplanes fly, we automatically assume that to go up you pull and to go down you push. Everyone learns sooner or later that the truth is that to go up you pull and to go down you pull some more (that's an old pilot joke). But until that knowledge is manifested in a reflex to push when the angle of attack is dangerously high, every pilot is a ticking time bomb. If every pilot had the training to use rudder to keep a wing from dropping at high angles of attack and to get the nose down when in doubt, we probably wouldn't have the classic stall-spin wrecks that occur. Many rated pilots don't realize the importance of coordination and the fact that a perfectly coordinated airplane will not spin when it stalls. It's the skid that turns into a spin and no pilot should be without that knowledge. Dale Masters, a talented glider pilot and author of "Soaring: Beyond the Basics", has rightly pointed out that slips are pretty benign but skids can be killers. He's also pointed out that, in his opinion, there is never a need to skid. No skid, no spin. Although I do practice and teach some skidding maneuvers, I can't fault Dale's logic.

ON-COURSE DESCENDING SLIPS

Now that we've mastered all this air work it's just about time to work on landings. So it's probably a good time to become proficient at the maneuver that will often help us to accurately put the plane on the spot of ground we've selected.

Many pilots are fairly familiar with the forward slip. But others couldn't pull off a good forward slip if their life depended on it. Well, it might, so that's why it's so important. It's the most effective way to steepen the glide of an aircraft not equipped with flaps or spoilers and can be used in addition to those controls in most aircraft.

Here are two ways to look at the forward slip entry: One is that we apply rudder to present the side of the plane to the relative wind and apply a sufficient amount of opposite aileron to hold the course constant. The other is to bank the plane to the desired amount and apply a sufficient amount of rudder to hold the course constant. Either way, the result is the same. Because we present the side of the plane to the relative wind, the drag is dramatically increased, allowing a steepening of the glide without an attendant increase in airspeed. In practical application, most pilots will apply aileron and rudder simultaneously and make adjustments to each during the descending slip. By now you know that I like to simplify things and I've found that the forward slip is easiest when we just bury the rudder to the stop. There, we just eliminated one variable. With the rudder buried, we need only vary bank angle to control our course. In most airplanes you'll find that if you raise the nose you'll get a little more rudder authority. I believe it's because with the resultant decrease in airspeed the vertical stabilizer has less of a stabilizing influence. (I'm still researching this. I never said I had all the answers.)

We won't always bury the rudder. Let me explain why: We are always preparing ourselves for the dead stick emergency landing into the tiny little field. Once more let's steal a good idea from the glider guiders. Gliders make dead stick landings all the time and most glider pilots use a technique that makes it easier to make an accurate spot landing. Early in their pattern, say about midfield downwind, they pop some spoilers, maybe about twenty-five percent. At that setting they try to fly a pattern, which will put them on the target. But when on final they might find that they are too high. No problem, they just extend more spoiler to steepen the approach. If they find that they are too low to reach the point of intended touchdown they simply retract what spoilers they already have. The result is like opening a throttle. Their descent shallows and the glide is extended. It's because of this capability that gliders can be landed so accurately.

We'll use the forward slip technique just like the glider pilot uses his spoilers. We'll treat the depressed rudder pedal like the glider's spoiler lever. Remember, this is a constant course maneuver, and the amount of aileron needed to maintain our course will be in direct proportion to the amount of rudder we depress. We'll practice dead stick approaches with a little cross-control to steepen the approach. If it's not steep enough we can increase the degree of forward slip. If it looks like we're going to land short we can clean the airplane up by returning to more coordinated flight and extend our glide

We'll use alternating descending forward slips as a practice maneuver. Beginning with a high pattern, we'll turn a high long final approach. Then we'll kick the airplane into a forward slip with one wing down. Once stabilized with course constant, we'll kick it around until the other wing is down. Once stabilized in that slip, we'll kick it again to the original side. We'll just keep alternating those slips until it's time to straighten the ship out for touchdown. But we still might not be done forward slipping.

I believe that the most graceful forward slip entry is the one entered while in the turn from base to final. It warms the cockles of my little black heart to see this done well.

Let's say that at the key position[7] we determined that we were high. We would start the turn from base to final. Taking advantage of the fact that the aircraft is already banked for that turn, we'd simply add opposite rudder to cause the forward slip. Bank is still used to turn the plane, regardless of heading. Because of the opposite rudder being used, we may find that a little steeper bank may be necessary to maintain the necessary turn rate to accurately intercept the extended center line of the

---

[7] *The key position is where you find yourself immediately after turning from downwind to base. It is important because it's where you make an important judgment as to your ability to glide accurately to the touchdown point.*

runway.

I've discovered that a lot of pilots can't enter a slip properly while flying a right-hand pattern. Why not? Because they've gotten into the habit of entering a slip on final and have always dropped their left wing. If asked to enter a slip while in a right turn, they will attempt to drop their left wing. It doesn't work. But it tells me a lot about their training and it's okay... we'll fix it.

The absolutely easiest, funnest, coolest and most efficient way to enter a forward slip is in the turn from base to final. As you reach the 45 degree point in this turn you are already banked. Simply add outside rudder to start your forward, but turning, slip. As you apply rudder the bank will want to decrease so you'll have to add more aileron. You will also continue to use bank to control the turn rate and final course. As you roll out on final, continue to hold rudder and use aileron to keep your position on the extended centerline. Wasn't that easy?

But wait! There's more! Most pilots assume that the purpose of the forward slip is to steepen the descent without increasing speed. It certainly does that. But if you are carrying too much airspeed, simply stay in the slip as you round out at the bottom of the descent. Stay in the slip as you flare. You will lose speed more efficiently and land shorter. With practice you'll be able to judge when to kick out of the slip. Obviously you want to kick out before touching down (it helps to practice this on a dirt strip, so that if you touch down while in the slip, the result won't cause any harm). This is a really valuable use for the slip. I know because I've used it lots of times to prevent what would otherwise have been an embarrassingly long landing!

I think that practicing these slips will give you a lot of confidence so that, when the time comes, you'll be able to stuff that plane into the driveway of the sewage treatment plant and walk away from it smelling like a rose.

ARE YOU WORKING TOO HARD?

Many of these maneuvers we're practicing can be very challenging and by now you may have worked up a sweat. So it might be a good time to ask yourself if you're working too hard at this stuff.

When I was becoming re-current in gliders I flew with Kat Haessler in the venerable 2-33 two-place trainer. I thought I was doing a fine job of flying precisely when Kat asked, "Jeez, what are you trying to do, churn butter?" She was referring to all the inputs to the aileron and elevator I was busy making. Her point was that the long-winged 2-33 has such a low roll rate that you could cut your rolling inputs in half and probably not make a bit of difference in the ship's attitude. I was working too hard. You'll find a couple of references to this phenomenon in subsequent sections. It becomes most noticeable when we are setting up to land. We'll fly along quite happily on the downwind without a lot of control inputs. But let us get close to the ground on short final and suddenly we're moving that stick like crazy, trying to precisely control our craft close to the ground. Half those control inputs probably aren't necessary. So, as Kat would snidely advise, "quit churning butter".

THE EXPOSUROMETER: EVERY PILOT SHOULD HAVE ONE

While we've been flying around practicing all these fun maneuvers have you been paying attention to what's underneath us? Is it the kind of terrain on which we can land without hurting ourselves too badly?

In my opinion far too many single engine pilots fly with little or no regard for the consequences of an engine failure or other emergency requiring an immediate landing. It's not that I don't think there are times you should be willing to fly over inhospitable terrain. It's just that I think most pilots have grown complacent about the reliability of engines.

Mountain climbers refer to the amount of risk of each part of a climb as "exposure". The term is perfect and every pilot should have an "exposurometer" in his head.

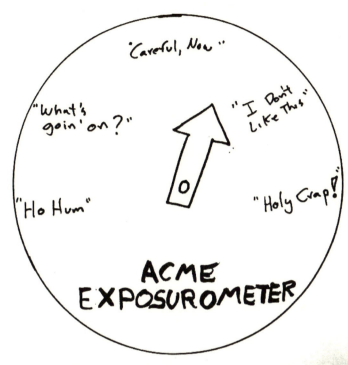

Flying at altitude over Kansas in clear weather, the instrument would rest at "Ho-hum". Flying over, say Bryce Canyon in Utah at low altitude, the needle would be pegged on "Holy Crap" and a horn would be sounding, or maybe one of those cool recordings of a voice calmly intoning, "Warning: You are an idiot. There is no place to put this crate down below you, no place within gliding distance and, at this altitude, no time to pick the least horrible place to land. I repeat, you are an idiot..." Perhaps we could punctuate that announcement with some sort of sound effect; a bell, a gong, a klaxon... aw forget it, the voice alone will do.

I'm not saying that a single engine pilot should never fly over something on which he'd rather not land. There are times you just play the odds and the odds really are in our favor. I just think you're a fool not to be constantly aware of how great your exposure is.

ENGINE FAILURE (GULP!)

Earlier we talked about instinctively lowering the nose in the event of engine failure. That is certainly an appropriate action if we are at a high angle of attack, but it may not be the proper action in every gait. Let's see if we can refine our reaction to an engine failure. We need to review what we will do in regard to conserving altitude and what our actions will be to restore power if that's possible.

If you were at cruise speed and only fifty feet off the ground when the engine packed it in, you certainly wouldn't lower the nose, would you? The proper course of action would be to RAISE the nose in order to trade excess airspeed for much needed altitude. My point is that I'd like to see every pilot develop the reflex to change his angle of attack appropriately for every condition of speed and altitude in which he might find himself when the engine quits.

Once that first reaction has been made, an attempt should be made to restore power if possible. Some instructors would counsel that, time permitting, this action can be limited to changing fuel tanks, selecting carburetor heat and rich mixture. They are concerned that an attempt to restore power may interfere with a successful power-off landing. I agree. Some instructors would also counsel that when the decision has been made to land, the throttle should be closed so that if the engine comes to life it won't louse up the accuracy of your approach. It's a reasonable point. Everyone should have a quick little mental checklist that they can sail into if an engine quits. It can certainly be as simple as "change fuel tanks, pump on, mixture rich, carb heat on".... Personally, I am real fond of the first item being first.

As is often the case, you are well advised to have planned ahead and drilled for this emergency in order to eliminate the need to figure it all out when it happens. One thing you can count on: If you ever have an engine failure followed by an emergency landing, every airport bum around will second-guess everything you did and, from the comfort of their recliners in the pilots' lounge, criticize your every move.

Now that we've handled that little emergency, let's head for the airport.

INBOUND

Just a quick word here about efficiently descending to our destination. I mainly teach in airplanes with fixed pitch propellers. I can't tell you how many pilots have demonstrated the disturbing technique of bringing the power way back (below the green arc) in order to descend to pattern altitude. The airplane's speed will remain pretty much the same as it descends. This seems to me to be terribly inefficient. How 'bout we use the fourth "gait" of cruise descent? We simply lower the nose. Then, as the RPM starts to increase, we reduce the power in order to maintain the RPM. Basically, we're decreasing manifold pressure in order to maintain the same RPM we had at cruise. You'll quickly figure out how much to reduce the throttle in order to both maintain RPM and a reasonable descent rate. I like about 500 Feet Per Minute because it's easy on most people's ears. Depending on temperature and humidity, you may choose to select carburetor heat before reducing the manifold pressure. There is a phrase I find myself using just as much as "more right rudder" or "keep it straight". That is "Carb heat is your first power reduction". It's more appropriate to airplanes powered with Continental engines.   Lycomings normally don't have as great a need. Your first flight instructor must have taught you to select carburetor heat while the manifold is hot, not after you've reduced the power and cooled the exhaust. I don't know why so many pilots have forgotten that basic technique.

WATER SKIING

On our way back to the airport we pass over a nice, deserted lake. It beckons to us.

"C'mon, you two, stick your wheels in my water. You know you want to", it seems to say.

Water skiing, or hydroplaning an airplane, is one of those things that just tempts the bejabbers out of the adventurous pilot. Don't teach yourself to do it. And don't listen to the Geezer Patrol with their admonitions of whether or not to apply the brakes when the wheels are wet. Those who know the secrets of water skiing will never discuss silly things like brakes. If you take my course and play your cards right, I might give you some water skiing dual. Otherwise stay away from that tempting wet playground.

The photo below shows my friend Jerry Groendyke and me skiing my Cub on the Intracoastal Waterway between Georgia and Florida. Jerry's flying... I'm just going along for the ride. Jerry talked me into doing this. I relented in a moment of weakness. It was all Jerry's fault. Jerry and my friend George DeMartini are the only really good pilots I know who worked for the FAA. I'm sure there are others... I just don't know them.

Playing with a Cub on the St Marys River

THE PATTERN

Let me start this section with one of my favorite subjects for a rant: Flying to a point from which to enter the downwind on a 45 degree angle. I realize that if we all fly the same pattern it contributes toward an orderly (and maybe safer) gaggle of flying folks arriving, but this particular practice is just nuts in my opinion. The way I see it, entering on a 45 only makes sense when you are inbound within about a forty or fifty degree arc of that entry. Sunriver, Oregon has right traffic for runway 18. I see people come in from the East and fly literally miles away to turn around and enter on that 45. I guess that's why I like the overhead approach so much. If you aim for the center of the airport at a little above pattern altitude and enter from a descending turn, you'll have the benefit of being able to spot most other traffic as well as the wind sock and you won't be going clear out to East Moosebreath in order to turn around and come back.

I'm convinced that the reason this 45 degree nonsense is being taught goes right back to minimum standards, right along with the "stabilized approach" and that old wheeze, "the key to a good landing is a good approach". You should be able to execute a good landing out of ANY approach, especially a short approach and if you must have the extra time and room that the miles-away 45 entry gives you, then perhaps you should take up a slower-moving activity like moss-growth-observation.

I'll take it a step further: Maybe this shouldn't be your normal procedure, but you should be able to fly a downwind no further away from the runway than the distance from which you can do a 180 degree turn at 80 degrees of bank and in a descent so that you touch down immediately upon rolling out of that 180. That is a reasonably do-able maneuver and if you can't do it you better start practicing. Okay, done with rant. More about that high-performance and efficient approach at the end of this section.

The airport traffic pattern is a place where you'll see clear differences between the SRMC[8] trained pilot and everyone else.

A lot of conventionally trained pilots really get upset if they see another pilot straying from the established pattern. Most of their anger is due to a phenomenon I call "aviation pretentiousness syndrome", or APS[9], but some of their displeasure can be justified. After all, traffic pattern protocol was established to safely separate all the planes using that airport and to make it possible to predict what the guy in front of you is probably going to do. During a SRMC flight in a busy pattern, we may have to compromise to a certain extent in order to fit in. Here are a few of the ways in which we differ from other pilots in the pattern:

We use the radio sparingly. We might communicate directly with another plane in the pattern so he'll know what we're doing[10], but normally our calls are limited to a call on downwind. We have an absolute distrust for the radio as a means of detecting traffic. We depend on vision. For more on the radio, see a subsequent tirade entitled "The Radio".

We fly a much smaller and lower pattern than normal. The reasons are threefold: safety, economy and quality of training. As previously mentioned, we are always interested in keeping our exposure to a minimum. A straight climb on takeoff sometimes results in flight over inhospitable terrain, while a turn at a couple of hundred feet or less will keep us either over the field or with fewer degrees of turn required to get back to it. That's why you must always be willing to adapt your pattern to the circumstances, something most conventionally trained pilots are unwilling to do. Let me give you an example of a situation in which a non-standard pattern is clearly called for: I occasionally fly in and out of a grass strip on one of Georgia's barrier islands. The strip runs diagonally through a large pasture, which is surrounded by trees. I am often near max gross weight when

---

[8] *Stick and Rudder Master Class. This is a course I rarely teach any more. It contains all the advanced maneuvers featured in Brian's Flying Book.*

[9] *A huge percentage of pilots have adopted the attitude that what they do is really serious, really skillful and that they, therefore, are really important. Humility is not their strong suit. Driving a car is potentially more dangerous. I've found that the tendency toward APS is inversely proportionate to piloting skill. These pilots need to get over themselves.*

[10] *That call might be something like, "pardon us, but we're going to go in front of you. We are not cutting you off. You will not have to alter your normal approach."*

departing. With the wind out of the East, a takeoff would carry me across the pasture, then over a forested area until I reach the beach and the ocean. A conventionally trained pilot would climb straight ahead until about four hundred feet before starting any turn. That course would put him at an unacceptably low altitude over the trees. I simply use common sense to keep my exposure to a minimum. As soon as my tires leave the ground I make a right turn to the southern edge of the pasture. Then I turn left and proceed to follow the edge of the pasture as I climb. At no time am I exposed to the danger of landing in the trees. If the engine quits right after takeoff I can land straight ahead; if it quits after my right turn I can land alongside the tree line or convert airspeed to distance and get back to the strip. At no time am I out of gliding distance to the field. Once high enough, I can leave my course along the tree line and safely cross the forest because I am within gliding distance to the field or the beach.

Many airports are laid out as triangles. On such an airport you can, theoretically, take off and make an early turn toward the inside of the airport as you climb. Such a pattern will keep you within gliding distance of a runway until you are high enough to begin a climb on course... if you keep turning.

My rule for creating patterns is simple. If you takeoff and find yourself with no place to go straight ahead in the event of engine failure, TURN! Especially if you are only a couple of hundred feet or less, why should you continue over Nastyland when you can climb out within gliding distance to the field from which you departed? Instructors teach their students a rule of never trying to get back to the runway in the event of an engine failure and that the straight ahead landing in control is preferable to the possible stalling-turn-fireball of death. That's a sage rule for a default plan if we haven't planned for an engine failure or for the pilot who can only herd the airplane around, but we're training pilots who are in much more precise control. A pilot with common sense and good training will avoid exposure with an early turn and will also know at what altitude he can execute a dead-stick 270/90 degree turn back to the runway. Practice it at altitude and find out.

A long, straight-out climb in a closed pattern is the first leg of a pattern that cheats students both economically and in quality of instruction. The student flying the normal pattern will be droning around for four to six minutes, after which he will get one touch and go landing. Worse, he might be asked to stop and taxi back! A more appropriately sized pattern will take less than two minutes to complete and we'll make sure that you get several touchdowns or some one-wheel practice for your trouble. Do the math: The average student is getting a fraction of the practice for his training dollar. It works out even better for the more experienced pilot taking the SRMC. Due to your higher proficiency you'll learn even more than the less experienced pilot.

We'll utilize several different patterns including the abbreviated standard pattern, the back and forth pattern, the round-robin-every-runway-there-is pattern and others. But the only time we can utilize all of them is when the airport is otherwise deserted. With too much other traffic your unusual patterns can be somewhat disruptive if not used judiciously.

You might find that you'll have to establish some new habits while in the pattern. Since it's vitally important that we maintain visual contact with any other traffic we must constantly be looking for it. That's why it's important that we clear our space before every turn. We'll do this either by raising the inside wing before the turn (sort of a single-cycle Dutch Roll) or by making a rapid roll to a steep turn and looking through the greenhouse window.

Make a habit of looking up the final approach course before starting your turn from base to final. You may spot the guy who's making a straight-in approach or the guy finishing up a 747 pattern with a resultant two-mile final leg. And don't forget the guy who may be marching to a different drummer. I once had an extremely close call because I failed to see a guy on right base about to turn final while I (and the rest of the world) was on left base about to turn final. With all my usual looking around I had missed the guy right in front of me!

On a sunny day keep a lookout for shadows. I can't tell you how often I've spotted traffic because their shadow tipped me off to their presence.

And a word about wind: Know where the wind is. I'm always amazed at how many "pilots" totally ignore the wind. At an airport with a windsock you should check it on downwind and again on short final just to know what to expect. On takeoff you should check the sock before you add power. Don't minimize wind. It is our medium and we must know what it's doing.

A WORD ABOUT MANNERS

This might be a good spot to discuss how we behave when we all come together in one spot like the traffic pattern. Why is it that when on a sidewalk we are polite, offering the right of way to others and often using phrases like, "excuse me" and "after you". We tend to be far less polite when in cars or planes. Let me share with you an event that made a big impression on me:

It was a pretty good soaring day. We'd gotten off tow at about 6,500 feet and had gradually worked our way up to 8,500 or so. I was flying with a friend who is a pretty good stick. He'd decided to get an added glider rating and had come to get some instruction. We were flying the big yellow 2-32 in which I flew rides. He was doing a pretty good job of staying in lift and I was leaving him alone to get comfortable in this relatively new kind of flying. I was happy to be flying with someone who was demonstrating good stick and rudder skills. Then I heard the radio.

"Aircraft at the intersection, this is Cherokee one two three alpha hotel (I made up the "N" number and think it's appropriate). I'm on final, please don't enter the runway."

It wasn't a terribly unusual call, and I still wasn't paying much attention to it. I could look down on the airport from my perch and see that the pilot who was the intended recipient of the call must not have heard it because he entered the runway and was on the roll.

The Cherokee pilot who I had first heard was suddenly deeply offended that someone had ignored his presence (and more importantly his radio calls) and entered the runway ahead of him.

"Cherokee one two three alpha hotel is going around to avoid that idiot in front of me!"

Now, **that** got my attention. What followed were a few more transmissions berating the NORDO aircraft departing. The Unicom operator got sucked into the conversation. I don't know why; it wasn't his problem but he loved to talk on the radio. And he was someone to whom the Cherokee pilot could complain. After a few more protestations and insults on the part of the Cherokee pilot, I keyed my mic:

"Gentlemen, let's discuss this on the ground".

I didn't identify myself. Transmissions stopped and that was the end of the diatribe.

I had been happy in the tranquility of my soaring. The radio had been a necessary interruption to that tranquility. At a reasonable volume I'm used to it and it doesn't bother me. But that Cherokee pilot had really pissed me off and now I found that I was angry. I wasn't angry at the "idiot" in that unidentified departing aircraft. He had operated legally without an operating radio at an uncontrolled airport without a lot of traffic. He had made one mistake. He failed to see the approaching Cherokee before he took the runway. Had he looked up-range for traffic? One of my crew at the intersection saw him taxi out and said that he did look both ways. Did he have a radio with the volume turned down so that he thought he had comms? I don't know. No one heard a transmission. He may have made one mistake that many of us have made and many more will make, but that's not the point. Safety wasn't the issue. No one was put in harm's way. The departing pilot wasn't the villain. In my opinion that Cherokee pilot was unmistakably the villain. He made his approach with the other aircraft in sight. With no communications coming from that aircraft, he should have been prepared for a runway incursion. His anger at having to initiate a go-around was un-called for. His rudeness and willingness to discuss the perceived slight on the radio was inexcusable. Actually, I think he enjoyed this chance to be dramatic, not realizing that he was being a dramatic jerk. He was a prime example of Aviation Pretentiousness Syndrome. His mother and his flight instructor should both be ashamed of him... or themselves if they allowed that kind of behavior.

Aviation can bring out the worst in many people. Years ago, the Disney Studio made a driving safety cartoon featuring Goofy (my hero) as a guy who, as "Mr. Walker", is mild mannered, kind and sweet. But when he gets in his car he becomes "Mr. Wheeler", an angry misanthropic individual who hollers at everyone in his way and is the archetypical source of "road rage". Many pilots become "Mr. Wheeler" when in an aircraft. They feel that they are incredibly important because they fly (they probably wear large watches). They feel that anyone who doesn't follow the rules that **they** learned is incompetent. The flying world is full of them. They are fools.

Don't expect other pilots to cooperate with your planned flight. You can't change their operations whether or not they are ill-advised. But you **CAN** alter **YOUR** behavior and the way you handle unexpected situations. A go-around is not an emergency and someone "cutting you off" is not a slap in the face. Go-around if you must. Prepare for the unexpected situations that can arise and pride yourself on the ability to do so with skill and equanimity. If you can't alter your plan without getting upset about it, perhaps you should pursue a different method of transportation. That Cherokee pilot may have thought the other pilot was an "idiot", but in my opinion that Cherokee might as well have been towing a banner which said "IDIOT" with an arrow pointing at the plane towing it. He probably dines with his hat on, too.

THE ABBREVIATED APPROACH

As promised, here's the approach to land that I favor, although I can't always do it because of traffic considerations: One of the major advantages to flying from one point to another is speed. We can fly from Portland to Bend in less than a third of the time we can drive it. In keeping with our quest for efficiency, it would behoove us to waste as little time as possible in the landing pattern. Traffic permitting, it would be most efficient if we could simply descend to a point from which a minimum-radius turn would end with us at approach speed right in front of our point of intended touchdown, just above the runway. I like to be able to use "cruise descent" to the point from which I turn short final, close the throttle and touch down. This technique flies in the face of the theory of "a good landing depends on a good approach". But it does conform to my belief that a properly trained pilot does not need to depend on a "good approach" to make a good landing. If you take either my Master Class or Tailwheel Endorsement Course, I'll give you a chance to practice it.

THE RADIO

You may want to skip this section because I'm going to climb on my soap box again for a moment. This little tirade will anger over half the pilots flying out there, but I'm sorry. I can't go with the herd when it comes to radio use, or what I believe to be mis-use.

I'm convinced that the radio is an over-used and over-relied-upon device. Over-used because far too many needless transmissions are made which clutter the airwaves; over relied upon because it's common usage causes many pilots to assume that all traffic is reporting or reported. That's why during the Stick and Rudder Master Class I encourage you to re-think what you may have been taught about the use of the radio.

Let me give you an example of the type of radio usage that I object to: When approaching an un-controlled field, the average pilot will call the Unicom and request a traffic or airport advisory.

The average Unicom is not closely attended, so he will have to make this call several times. While he's plaintively calling the Unicom for an airport advisory, I'm trying to talk a guy through his first wheel landing. It's not easy because our intercom communications are being interrupted by this guy who's evidently never heard of a windsock. Finally the fifteen year-old son of the FBO owner wanders over to the radio. He looks at the electric wind direction indicator, which happens to be momentarily stuck 180 degrees out of kilter, then tells the arrival what runway to use. The arrival is now happy as a clam because he's received an "advisory" from a stranger of unknown qualifications. He still doesn't know for sure which way the wind is blowing or what traffic is in what pattern (The advisories at a certain resort airport in Central Oregon always include an altimeter setting which you probably don't need and never include a traffic advisory that you do need). He comes blasting into the pattern on a forty-five and calls that entry: "Cessna Niner Three Four Yankee Zulu is on a forty five for the left downwind to runway three-two at Moosebreath Municipal". Then he makes a similar call on downwind, base and on final. He runs out of control effectiveness right after touching down in a 20 knot tailwind and wonders why that landing was such a rodeo. Finally to end his broadcast day, he calls "Cessna Niner Three Four Yankee Zulu is clear of the active at Moosebreath Municipal".

Let's review how silly the preceding scenario was: To begin with, he'd have been better off to monitor the frequency from a ways out, make a quick position and intention report and maybe **one** request for an advisory, then cross over the field at 1,500 feet AGL or so in order to scope out the windsock, landing direction indicators on the segmented circle and other traffic besides that heard on the radio (I estimate that about a quarter of Unicom stations are actually manned. Multiple requests for advisories are often unanswered). Then he could have entered the pattern by descending into the left crosswind or downwind leg and make just one call, "Moosebreath Traffic, Skylane left downwind three-two, Moosebreath". By the way, it sometimes helps to say where on the downwind you are. I like reporting at the midfield so everyone knows where I am. I once heard a guy report every leg and he reported twice, about a minute apart. I finally had to ask him just exactly WHERE he was! Back to

Moosebreath: By omitting his N number he shortened his call. No one needs to know it (N numbers are only good for ordering fuel and reporting real or imagined violations to the Feds) and it's more important to identify yourself as to type or model. Now others in the pattern know to look for a 182. This method is even more useful when you're flying something like a "Yellow Cub" or a "Biplane". I was once far from home and approaching an airport in Canada. I heard a call on the CTAF. A female voice announced: "Canuck traffic, biplane on left downwind, runway three-two". It was unmistakably my pal, Suzanne Oliver, in the Pepsi Travelaire skywriting biplane. There was no mistaking what to look for and there was clearly no reason to use an "N" number in that perfectly succinct call.

Here's an interesting wrinkle on that practice that is a recent and annoying one to me. When Cessna bought Columbia, many new Columbia pilots began referring themselves as "Cessna" in their radio calls. I was flying my Pawnee towplane off of Sunriver when I heard a guy call, "Sunriver traffic, Cessna 1234 Uniform is four miles north straight in to runway 18." I started looking for a Cessna. Eventually I spotted a low wing aircraft but still couldn't locate that pesky Cessna, and I was easing my way into the pattern. A call to that "Cessna" to find out where he was revealed that the low-wing I had spotted was the "Cessna". Since then, I've heard it several times and no one seems to know, or care, how confusing this practice is.

Often an airport shares its Unicom or CTAF frequency with others in the area, so you listen to their traffic whether you want to or not. By beginning the call with the airport name, we enable the guys at other airports to ignore the rest of our transmission while alerting anyone at Moosebreath that we are in their pattern. We state the runway so traffic will know where we are going to land. We end the transmission with the name of the airport because it's often the case that other traffic "stepped on" the first part of our call with their own cockpit conversation. By ending with it, those guys will know where we are and whether they need to take note. Under normal circumstances no other calls are necessary unless there's a high volume of traffic and we need to make sure we're being seen. We will taxi off the runway maintaining our silence. Licensed pilots have to pass medical exams which include vision tests. A guy who needed to be told that we were clear of the active would also have to have a Braille checklist (I did see a Braille menu at the drive-up window at a McDonalds once). "Clear of the active" is the most useless of all transmissions except under rare circumstances.

There is currently another controversy raging over the use of the phrase, "other traffic, please advise". It seems there's a faction that thinks this call is really horrible and should never be used. I think they've got their heads wedged. There's nothing wrong with making this blind call to ask others who might be a factor to speak up and let you know they're there. Otherwise they might not let you know. I use this call all the time when taking the runway for glider hookups so that I know I have enough time to hookup the glider and launch. So don't listen to those curmudgeons who object to it. Most people consumed with radio usage don't fly very well anyway.

Departure calls can be important, depending on the layout of the airport. While not really necessary at an airport with just one runway, it can be important to call your departure at a field with intersecting runways. I once had a near-miss with a corporate jet that could have been avoided had I made a departure call. I clearly had my own head wedged at the time and I'm still embarrassed by it. I was in "hurry up" mode, which is often a precursor to disaster. I had turned my radio on at the last minute and we were departing on runways whose departure ends intersected. Greater vigilance would also have prevented the incident if I had been without a radio.

But back to the airwaves over sleepy little Moosebreath Municipal: While we were arriving, the airwaves were, for the most part, quiet. Quiet so that instructors and students could hear each other on intercoms. Quiet so that hangar flyers in the FBO lobby could recount daring exploits without interruption. And quiet so that someone who had something really important to say could get a word in edgewise.

My students sometimes wonder why I'm often pulling the

squelch knob out to check the volume. One of the most common screwups pilots make is turning the volume down for one reason or another, then failing to turn it back up. The results of this little mistake are transmissions that block other people and a belief that one has communication when one only has transmission ability. The only thing worse than no radio is mistaken belief that you **HAVE** a working radio. Why do I check this item so often? Because I've made this mistake. In fact, I've made it several times. Usually it was because I was trying to communicate with a student or a crewman and the chatter on the radio was driving me nuts. So I turned it down and forgot to turn it back up. This practice can have some very serious repercussions. So, please check your volume from time to time to ensure that you can receive as well as transmit.

Speaking of radios, let's talk about...

THE STRAIGHT- IN APPROACH

For years, I've urged others to avoid the straight-in approach. The reason was that the guy making a straight-in is in a position to interrupt those making a conventional pattern with a base leg. With a few airplanes operating with no radios, this type of approach could create a conflict, if not a mid-air.

A while back I was in the pattern with a student when a guy called in that he was making a straight-in to the same runway we were using. Unfortunately, his approach would have brought him to the same spot as us. We called our position, but it didn't seem to make any difference to him. He just kept on coming. We figured that he must be on an urgent mission to justify cutting off an airplane that was already in the pattern, so we slowed to minimum controllable airspeed and let him go ahead of us. Then we fell in behind. You can imagine my surprise when the fellow did a touch and go and beat feet. It was the first time in a long time that I've been "cut off" in the pattern (I feel that most "cut offs" are imagined).

Interestingly, thinking about that incident is what has caused me to change my mind about straight-ins. I think they are okay. Times have changed. There are very few NORDO airplanes and a cautious pilot should be able to conduct a straight-in and spot any conflicting traffic. Also, I've noticed a tendency among many pilots who use this approach to call their position and intention and add, "traffic permitting". I figure that's the same as saying, "let me know if I'll be cutting you off and I'll do something else". That works for me. I've previously criticized approaches that waste time. You certainly can't get much more efficient than a straight-in approach.

Okay, if you skipped that section you can start reading again because now we're going to talk about...

LANDINGS

Landings are, for most pilots, the most difficult thing they have to learn. Landings are also the one operation on which the non-pilot passenger judges the skill of the pilot. I believe that perhaps landings wouldn't be such a big deal if we concentrated from the beginning on more precise control of the airplane. If you've spent your flying career herding airplanes around, landings will require precision that will tax your ability. But all the air work we do in the SRMC has required very precise control, so landings will not be as hard. That's why we can increase the degree of difficulty to a level that other pilots would never attempt. You'll really discover how precise you can be when you start practicing one-wheel work, but first we have to address the properties of the tailwheel equipped airplane that make it more difficult to handle on the ground than the more modern nose wheel equipped airplane.

THE ESSENCE OF THE TAILWHEEL AIRPLANE

The taildragger sits on its tailwheel as well as its mains because its center of gravity is behind the main wheels. When the airplane is in motion on the ground it's either accelerating (takeoff), decelerating (landing rollout) or rolling along at equilibrium (taxiing or practicing some of our ground maneuvers). When decelerating, the taildragger is at its most challenging because the center of gravity is behind the CENTER OF FRICTION (the center of friction is the point at which the airplane contacts the ground and as such is the point at which the force of friction between plane and ground is centered).

Have you noticed that contact with the air hardly ever hurts anyone? It's contact with the **ground** that can turn painful. So why are so many pilots so inept at controlling their airplanes when in contact with the ground? Many of the maneuvers I teach are designed to improve our skills at controlling the airplane in this awkward area when the airplane is operating in two mediums simultaneously, on the ground and in the air.

We're all familiar with the four forces that affect an airplane in flight (LIFT, WEIGHT, DRAG and THRUST), but it's especially important to understand the following forces and how they affect the airplane whenever it is in contact with the ground:

1. FRICTION between the airplane and the ground. This force is centered at the main wheels when they contact the ground. Although the tailwheel will sometimes be contacting the ground, its friction is much less than the mains. The direction of this force is not always straight back.

2. The WEIGHT of the airplane at its center of gravity. This is the point where the weight of the airplane is applied either through momentum or inertia.

3. THRUST. When power is applied it has a stabilizing effect on the plane because of its pulling force. It is the dominant stabilizing force. When that force is eliminated by closing the throttle, momentum at the center of gravity becomes the dominant force and it's far from stable.

KEEPING IT STRAIGHT

What's the main difference operationally between the taildragger and the trike? The taildragger wants to depart from its heading both when taking off and more when landing. It requires constant tending of the rudder to stay straight. I'm going to repeat myself a little bit here because more on this subject can be found in the description of the maneuver, "The One-Footed Takeoff". In our well-founded concern with keeping the airplane straight both on takeoff and landing, we tend to "fan" the rudder. We use lots of rudder and apply it back and forth while seeking to keep that pesky plane from departing off the centerline. I find that immediately following every landing touchdown I'm saying, "Keep it straight". In order to keep it straight it is much more important to use rudder in a timely fashion than it is to use lots of it. I've discovered that half the amount of rudder is more effective than all of it if used sooner. Bear that in mind as you practice.

COURSE AND HEADING

As we move into landings, a little review might be appropriate.

If you fly with me, you'll hear these two terms a lot: "Course and Heading". What you'll usually hear is "At the moment of touchdown, course and heading must be the same!" Course is the way the plane is traveling and heading is the way it is pointing. You may be saying, "Well, of course the plane has to be traveling in the direction it's pointing at the moment of touchdown", but in the cockpit, amid all the action during the flare, you may forget.

When a plane touches down with course different from heading it scrubs tires and sideloads the gear. The resultant friction causes a sudden, unexpected heading change, setting the scene for a ground loop. There are always forces at work to change the course and heading, even on a dead calm day. That's why a plane in a state of perfect coordination will rarely have perfectly matched heading and course at the moment of touchdown. **That's why you have to know how to cross-**

control and that's one reason the cross-control maneuvers taught in the Stick and Rudder Master Class are so important.

Remember that yayhoo next to you urging you to "keep it straight"? You might wonder, "Where IS straight?" In a tandem seated airplane it's pretty easy to judge where straight ahead lies. But in a side-by-side airplane, with its curved cowl and us sitting on either side of the centerline, it can be a little questionable. Most such airplanes that are equipped with control wheels have the shaft on which that wheel or yoke is mounted running parallel to the longitudinal axis, or centerline, of the plane. You're sitting right behind that yoke, so you can just use that shaft as your heading bug. First, make sure it actually IS aligned with the longitudinal axis of the plane.

THE HIGH SPEED FLARE

A lot is made about approach speed. The speed at which you "cross the fence" determines how long a landing you will make and how long it will take you to bleed off excess speed to either stall in a three-point or plant in a wheel landing. I've found that using a very high speed across the fence will sometimes help in the early stages of learning these two landing types. The high speed flare works because it stretches out the time it takes to stall or plant. That gives you more time to practice and to learn. You may find that it's a great idea to cross the fence at over 100 MPH in one of our little taildraggers just to slow the operation down a bit.

THE THREE-POINT LANDING

It could be said that the successful three-point landing is actually an unsuccessful attempt to keep from landing. Let me explain why:

If we fly our airplane to within two inches of the ground, reduce the power to idle and attempt to maintain our two-inch altitude using pitch alone, what will happen? Probably a really nice three-point landing. Airspeed will bleed off as we apply more and more up elevator to maintain our altitude. Eventually we will reach the stalling angle of attack with the stick all the way back. The airplane will quit flying and, since we're only two inches off the ground, it will settle to the ground with a gentle "plop". We will immediately have effective tailwheel steering because the full weight of the tail will be on the tailwheel (additional downward force will be exerted by the up elevator). We will also have some directional control from the rudder due to its movement through the relative wind.

The problems most people have with the three-point landing are: 1. Stalling too high. 2. Touching the ground before stalling. 3 Over controlling and creating a pilot-induced oscillation while flaring. 4. Directional control following the touchdown. The single most common student mistake is touching the runway before stalling.

I can't overemphasize the importance of maintaining altitude control throughout the flare. We may not be able to maintain that two-inch altitude mentioned before, but we can maintain enough control to stay within what I call a "landing window". The landing window is a range of altitude starting at just clear of the ground and extending up to the maximum height from which we can stall and drop the airplane in and not be ashamed of the resulting landing. It's usually about two feet but can be lower, depending on how proficient you are. If you can remain in that window without touching the ground until the stall pays off you will have an acceptable landing. I have found that most people are reluctant to apply enough backpressure toward the end of the flare and thus their biggest problem is touching down too soon. That's where bounced landings come from.

Remember that a successful flare is usually nothing more than an attempt to avoid landing by applying more and more back pressure until there's no more back pressure to apply.

To avoid oscillating during the flare sometimes requires a tool from our psychological toolbox. I call it "the Flaring Ratchet". George DeMartini is one of the best instructors I know and it's his idea that, on flaring to land, you should imagine that there is a ratchet-like device attached to the elevator. This device would limit movement of the elevator to "up". Every time you pulled back a little on the stick you'd feel a "click" and you wouldn't be able to move it forward again. Only back. You wouldn't be able to chase a pilot-induced oscillation back and forth. Using the ratchet, you'll find yourself being very careful not to ever pull back too far, so you probably won't start that PIO in the first place. The flaring ratchet: Keep one in your mental toolbox. I think George's flaring ratchet may have been what made me think up the one-footed takeoff, which I'll introduce later. Thanks, George.

Speaking of flares, one day Jeff Stanford and I were discussing the trials of teaching three-point landings. Jeff is a very talented instructor who owns a beautiful Taylorcraft L2 in which I did a bunch of instructing. We were agreeing that a major problem our students had was failing to have the stick all the way back to the stop at touchdown... and the fact that sometimes they thought they had it all the way back but, in fact, still had some room to go. We joked that it would be cool to have a micro switch on the elevator and a red light up on the top of the compass where it would be clearly visible. When the stick was back full the light would come on. A couple of days later I came out to fly with a new tailwheel student and found that Jeff had actually installed the device. We had a ball with that light. Every time someone would bounce a landing we could say, "Was the light on?" It seems a little silly, but it was a pretty good training aid and I'll bet that L2 is the only airplane in the world so equipped.

At touchdown in a taildragger you will have to deal with the problem of directional control. Remember, because the aircraft is decelerating, you are trying to throw a lawn dart tail first. The weight acting at the center of gravity wants to lead the rest of the mass down the runway. That weight can't go through the center of friction, which is on a line between the main wheels, so it tries to go-around it. That's what a ground loop is, a successful attempt by the weight at the center of gravity to go-around the center of friction. When you use rudder to keep the plane going straight down the runway you are doing the same thing as balancing a stick vertically on your finger. With no wind and a perfectly steady hand you wouldn't have to shift back and forth to balance the stick, but the slightest adverse force will upset equilibrium, making it necessary for you to work to balance that stick. And so you find that you will almost always have to work the rudder, making little corrections (and probably a lot of over-corrections) back and forth to keep the plane straight.

THE CURSE AND BLESSING OF TAILWHEEL STEERING

The overwhelming majority of tailwheel airplanes are equipped with a steerable tailwheel. The tailwheel assembly is like a caster on a shopping cart, free to turn about a pivot point. A pair of steering arms project from either side and are connected to the pivot. When the arms are connected to the rudder, usually by chains and springs, any movement of the rudder will be transmitted to the tailwheel. Thus if you push the right rudder pedal the rudder will move to yaw the airplane to the right and the tailwheel will rotate as well, causing the airplane to turn right on the ground. Pretty nifty, huh? Well, there is just one little wrinkle and that wrinkle can spoil your day. Let's say that you are in the process of landing three-point in a cross wind from the right. In order to stay over the center line, you bank the airplane to the right. To avoid turning right, you apply left rudder. You are in a typical crosswind sideslip. As long as you stay in the air everything is hunky dory. But as soon as the airplane's tailwheel touches the ground, its canted off tailwheel causes it to swerve to the left. You feel this swerve and immediately apply lots of right rudder to stop it. That's just what the ground loop monster has been waiting for you to do. Now the tailwheel steering to the right and the wind blowing from the right conspire to rapidly turn your plane into the wind. A ground loop has been initiated and only correct and timely applications of rudder and maybe brake will prevent the coming wreck.

I've always felt that the cure for this phenomenon was the correctly applied application of neutral rudder right before touchdown. I admit that it's tricky and complicates the already complicated process of the crosswind landing. And then I talked to Bill.

Bill Duncan, who owns "Alaskan Bushwheel", has certainly studied tailwheels as much as anyone. Bill feels that steerable tailwheels have been the reason for more ground loops than any other cause. The man owns a tailwheel manufacturing company and can put anything he wants on his Maule. He can also change his mind and change his tailwheel, which he probably has. Bill's Maule is equipped with a fully swiveling tailwheel with no steering.

I have always felt that a tailwheel airplane should have three methods of turning on the ground; rudder, brake and tailwheel steering. After talking with Bill, I may just change my thinking. But as long as I conduct tailwheel training I guess I should have tailwheel steering and teach the technique of neutralizing the rudder at the instant of touchdown in a three-point landing.

THE WHEEL LANDING

There is a certain amount of mystique surrounding the wheel landing. There is also a common feeling among aviators that the wheel landing is more difficult than the three-point. However, I'm sure that if I started a primary student doing wheel landings he'd progress a little faster than if I started him with 3-points.

First, a definition of what a wheel landing is: It's a landing technique where the airplane is flown onto the ground. The main wheels touch and the elevator is used to maintain the pitch attitude. After all, the front end of the airplane can't continue to descend once the mains contact the ground, but the tail can continue to descend. If the tail is allowed to continue its descent, the angle of attack will increase. Assuming any excess of airspeed, an increase in angle of attack will result in increased lift and the airplane will rise into the air once more. That's why the quick application of elevator (the "plant") to keep the tail from descending is so important.

The main difference between wheel and three-point landings is that lift is lost at or before touchdown in the three-point and after touchdown in the wheel landing. This difference will be important when we discuss the advantages of the wheel landing.

The wheel landing is practiced more often in the SRMC because the one-wheel work we do is initiated with a wheel landing. The wheel landing is fundamental to virtually all comedy runway maneuvers that you'll see in air shows. It is also the jump-off point for your development as a truly competent pilot, not just a tailwheel pilot.

The wheel landing consists of three parts, the SWOOP, the SINK and the PLANT. We'll start with the same approach as the three-point landing. We often use the high-speed approach for the same reason we used it during the three-point: It will slow things down and give us more time. We will SWOOP the airplane into the landing window (about five feet above the numbers). We'll then stop that swooping descent. We will also change our visual target. You see, when you were swooping, you were probably watching the runway numbers which were your target. But now you MUST change your visual target and focus on infinity and the horizon. Now start the second part of the wheel landing, the SINK. Instead of holding our altitude until the stall, we will work to establish a SINK rate which will result in an acceptable touchdown force. We're going to use our elevator to control the rate of sink to the ground. We're using the energy we stored in the form of airspeed by swooping.

You can actually establish what that sink rate is by holding your hand about two feet above a table top, then bringing it down to the surface at a rate you believe would result in a nice smooth wheel landing. Time the descent of your hand. Divide twenty-four (inches) by the number of seconds the descent took and you will have the sink rate in inches per second. This little exercise may seem silly at first, but I believe in visualization and I think that visualization of an eight inch-per-second sink rate will help when you practice in the airplane.

Now that we've established an acceptable sink rate, we must deal with what to do at the moment of touchdown. This is the PLANT and it is the critical point of the wheel landing. Once again we must avoid that old bugaboo, the bounce.

ANATOMY OF A BOUNCED LANDING

Remember where the center of gravity is in the taildragger: Behind the main wheels. So if the airplane is descending and the main wheels contact the runway they must stop descending. That's not true for the tail of the plane. Because of the configuration of the tailwheel aircraft, the tail of the plane is free to continue descending after the mains touch. If that is allowed to happen the angle of attack will suddenly increase. That will increase the amount of lift being generated and if the lift is greater than the weight of the aircraft, it will lift off the ground. We've got to keep that bounce from happening and we do that with "the PLANT".

PLANTING THE WHEELS

The perfect plant is precisely the right amount of forward elevator applied exactly at the moment the mains contact the ground. Learning that combination of TIMING and AMOUNT of forward pressure is one of the keys to learning the wheel landing. I'll give you a hint, though. The softer the touch, the less forward pressure must be applied and the less critical the timing of that application is. So if you want to learn to make great wheel landings, LEARN TO CONTROL YOUR SINK RATE!

The most common student mistake is failure to plant when the wheels touch. Some students occasionally display a very dangerous tendency to attempt a plant BEFORE the wheels touch. Don't ever do that. If you are very high off the ground and attempt a plant you will simply increase the sink rate and the landing will be hard. Just wait for the touch and be spring-loaded to the plant position.

THREE-POINT VS WHEEL LANDING

You can't be a taildragger pilot without getting sucked into the great WHEEL LANDING VS THREE-POINT LANDING DEBATE, so why don't we get into it right now. That way you'll be armed the next time you're in the airport bar hangar-flying with the Geezer Patrol.

There is a common misconception that a wheel landing is always done in close to a level flight attitude with resultant high speed. If that were true, then another misconception, that a three-point landing always results in a shorter landing, would also be true.

First, a wheel landing is simply a technique during which the mains are planted with the tail off the ground. It needn't be done in a level attitude. You can wheel land with the tail wheel one inch off the ground. Heck, you can turn a three-point landing into a wheel landing by immediately planting upon touchdown.

Second, a three-point landing is not necessarily a shorter landing than a wheel landing because those who make that argument forget about the role of brakes.

Let's say your airplane weighs 1,200 pounds and stalls at 40 MPH. If you land as short as you can in no wind, with a three-point landing you'll be rolling along the ground at something less than 40 MPH with your wings at a positive angle of attack and thus bearing a share of the plane's weight. As you apply your brakes they will not be nearly as effective as they would if the tires had the full 1,200 pounds resting on them. Now consider the same landing using the wheel landing technique. You may touch down at a slightly higher speed, say 45 MPH, but when you plant the wheels you instantly take all the weight off the wings and transfer it to the tires. Remember, both landings entail stopping 1,200 pounds but only the wheel landing has the advantage of 1,200 pounds worth of friction between the tires and the ground for added braking effectiveness.

The wheel landing really shines in a crosswind. Every airplane and every pilot have their maximum crosswind component. The wheel landing allows you to touch down at fairly high speed (and attendant control) in a brisk crosswind. As you gradually decelerate you will find whether or not you have the rudder authority to hold against the crosswind. If, as you slow down, you start losing lateral control you can either power up and go or use brake to keep additional steering. The point is that you find out gradually how you're doing against the crosswind. Were you to make a three-point landing you might find out all of a sudden that you don't have sufficient control right as you plunk it down in a stall with minimum effectiveness of all controls. Tailwheel steering also enters into the equation. The sooner the tail is firmly on the ground, the sooner tailwheel steering will be available to help keep the aircraft straight. However the effectiveness of tailwheel steering does vary between airplanes and tailwheels can be popped out of their steering detents and become useless for directional control. In gusting conditions there's no doubt that the wheel landing is the best choice because with additional speed there is additional control and you'll need it when the gusts keep changing your path through the relative wind

Why do so many pilots insist upon landing on the center line in a crosswind? Okay, I'll admit that I may have insisted on that for the sake of precision while training, but anytime you think that a crosswind might be getting a little close to your maximum, remember that you can always land diagonally on the runway, on a line which runs from the downwind side of the runway, across the centerline to the upwind side. That way you can shave a few degrees off the crosswind component. Just don't forget that you will eventually run out of runway on that heading!

WIND GRADIENT AND THE CROSSWIND LANDING

There's a rather annoying phenomenon that used to cause me problems during crosswind landings and then I noticed that it caused many of my students trouble. It's the effect of the wind gradient, the tendency of wind velocity to decrease as altitude decreases. On short final, at the point when we transition from crab to slip for crosswind correction we select just the right amount of bank angle to compensate for the crosswind. This bank angle will put our upwind wheel on the runway first. But as we descend to just above the runway the wind velocity decreases and we find that our bank angle is causing us to drift sideways into the wind. We have to stop that sideways drift so we bank the other direction, lowering our downwind wing. Then we touchdown with the wrong wheel first and sometimes even scrub the downwind tire from the outside in. Boy, did we screw up what started to be a very nice landing. The solution to the problem is easy: Just anticipate that decreasing crosswind and exercise restraint in correcting for any upwind drift. Remember the "Flaring Ratchet" for restraining the tendency toward pilot-induced oscillation? The principle is the same.

TOUCH AND GO OR FULL STOP?

This is a subject that'll really get the boys in the airport bar arguing. I think that each side has a valid point. We just have to use a little common sense to find a good compromise between safety, economy and quality of instruction.

The foes of touch and go landings will condemn them primarily on the grounds of safety. They will rightly point out that if you start a takeoff from a landing rollout you're leaving a lot of runway behind you and compromising the safety of your takeoff. They will also point out that a full stop landing more completely teaches and tests an ability to properly control the decelerating tailwheel airplane. They are right. Sort of.

The advocate of the touch and go landing will point out that a pilot using that method will get far more landings per hour and thus build his skills faster. He'll also point out that the advantage of the sheer number of landings far outweighs the relatively small disadvantage of not practicing the full stop and that he can always throw in a few full stops to make sure the student is becoming competent. He'll also point out that a takeoff from further down the runway is somewhat mitigated by the fact that the airplane is already rolling. Maybe for good measure he'll point out that if the landing is accurate and short the difference isn't that great.

I say that it all depends. It depends on the instructor, the student, the runway length, the wind and the traffic. If you're not smart enough to weigh all those considerations and make the right choice, you should be in the bar arguing and not out flying.

If we're all checked out on all these maneuvers and landing techniques, how 'bout we move into the hard stuff?

INTRO TO ONE-WHEEL WORK

There is, perhaps, one ability which really causes a well-trained and practiced pilot to stand out from the average ones and that's the ability to operate the airplane with just one-wheel touching the ground at a time. One-wheel work includes crosswind landings, slaloms back and forth on the runway and landings in a turn.

When I was still learning to fly, I saw Bill Warren put his J3 up on one-wheel and slalom the runway at an air show. It made a big impression on me. It was the first time I'd seen someone operate an airplane in this mode. The importance of the skill it demonstrated was not lost on me.

Although I normally like to see one-wheel work done with the wheel running true, in a no-wind situation we will often operate the plane on one-wheel during a prolonged high-speed taxi. In such a situation, the tire is going to scrub a little.

I often talk about the wheel "running true." "Running true" means that the course and heading of the airplane are the same and that the tire has no side load. That's a simple concept when we are on one-wheel in a crosswind. Then, the bank is holding us into the wind. Our course is right down the centerline and our heading is runway heading. In such a situation the airplane has to be on one-wheel to AVOID scrubbing a tire. Let's say the crosswind is from the left and we are on the left wheel with the right wheel about 12 inches from the ground. We'll probably be holding a little right rudder to keep the heading straight down the runway while we hold enough left aileron to keep the right wheel off the ground. We are clearly cross-controlled and if we were in the air we'd be uncoordinated (by the way, we will feel our upper bodies wanting to lean to the left as well). But because we are touching the ground and our tire is rolling straight with no side load, we're running true. Side load on the tire is the issue whenever we're touching the ground. In the example above, if we were to apply more right rudder than necessary, we'd also have to apply more left aileron to keep from turning right. We would then be traveling down the centerline with our nose to the right and our left tire being scrubbed sideways from the outside.

Running true is especially important (and harder to understand) when we are tracking a curve on one-wheel. The aircraft's heading and course are constantly changing in this condition, but they are still always equal.

LANDING IN A TURN

Okay, I admit it, this is one of my favorite maneuvers and it gives me warm fuzzies to see a student execute it with skill. It has the added value of being able to save your butt.

Analyzed, the landing in a turn is really quite simple. You just combine a wheel landing with a turn from base to final. Restated, you touch down during the turn from base to final. Since the airplane is banked and turning, you will touch down on one-wheel and be in a slalom style turn which will need to be followed by another turn the other direction if you don't want to run off the side of the runway. The key to a successful landing out of a turn is to visualize the track the airplane will take. I usually start the approach with a forty-five degree dogleg final leg so you're looking at the runway from a point forty-five degrees to one side. Once on that leg, you visualize where your track is going to be; you imagine that nice big arc and time your final approach so that you touch down somewhere in that arc. With practice you will be able to touch down at a pre-selected point on that imaginary arcing line.

Whuffos will look at our practice of the Landing in a Turn and shake their heads. They'll ask, "Now, what good can THAT maneuver possibly be?"

As you fly across this country, some of the features you'll notice a lot of are the irrigation pivots which dot the land from coast to coast. Their distinctive circles are easy to spot from the air and they represent a haven for a pilot flying a stricken airplane. However, most pilots using one of these circular pastures for an emergency landing will approach it on a straight line. They will attempt to land across it. They will discover the ruts made by the pivot's wheels. These wheel tracks can be as deep as a foot. In addition, they may also have berms thrown up by those wheels which may add another six inches or more on each side of that track. To cross those tracks is to invite catastrophe into what could have been a safe, uneventful landing. The pilot who both understands the layout of irrigation pivots and who is proficient in Landings in a Turn, will have no problem at all. He will simply land in a turn, staying inside the outermost wheel rut and outside the one directly inside it.

He'll need to know which way the wind is blowing and he'll need to use the pivot itself as his target so that his approach will clear the pivot by just twenty feet or so. That will ensure that his touchdown will occur with plenty of room in front of him so that he won't smack the same pivot on his rollout. The drawing below shows how the approach is made and the track that the plane makes. Please excuse the drawing quality it was drawn by a blind squirrel who, I think, had been drinking...

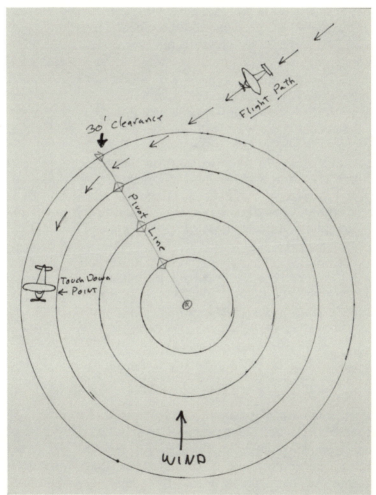

Even if you haven't had the opportunity to secure a property owner's permission and actually practice this maneuver, if you know how to make a landing in a turn and you follow these simple rules, you should be able to make such an emergency landing.

The landing in a turn may be a valuable emergency landing technique, but it is also a great way to introduce one-wheel work.

UP ON ONE-WHEEL

When you land in a turn it's easy to be on one-wheel because that's the way you first touch the ground. But getting up on one-wheel from a start is a little different. The first time I tried to get my Taylorcraft BC12D up on one-wheel I cranked in all the aileron I had and couldn't figure out why it didn't get up. Then the light bulb went on and I realized that aileron alone wasn't enough. The airplane's angle of attack had to be increased with the elevator in order to sufficiently lighten the aircraft to raise the wheel. Virtually every student I fly with has the same experience so I suggest that you put in all the aileron, then apply backpressure to get the wheel off. Naturally, as the airplane accelerates, you will need to back off on the aileron in order to maintain the bank and not let it increase as the wing increases lift and the aileron increases its authority. Failure to decrease aileron as the wheel comes off the ground is the most common error when you first start practicing.

Your initial one-wheel work will probably be in a straight line and we may not be running true in a headwind or no-wind condition. That's why I like to do this in the grass. That way any tire scrubbing we do will have little consequence.

THE SLALOM

You may have performed this maneuver before without meaning to. It's at the top of every air show comedy pilot's list of maneuvers guaranteed to make it look like he's out of control. But, to the contrary, it is a maneuver that, when properly performed, is exquisite to watch because it demonstrates total control of the aircraft in a mode where most pilots demonstrate very little control.

We will carve "S" turns down the runway on one-wheel at a

time. Each time we cross the centerline we will change wheels and then change direction.

Start the slalom with a wheel landing into the wind on one side of the centerline, let's say the right side. Then raise the right wheel off the ground and begin a curving course to the left. You'll need a power setting that will give you the right amount of speed for this maneuver. In both the 115 HP Cub and the 85 HP Cessna 140 we usually use about 1,700 RPM but you really don't want to be looking at the tach right now. Instead, listen to the engine and judge the speed required to give you both some roll authority and, more importantly a close to level pitch attitude.

You must know how steep you can bank before dragging a wingtip, so note a safe bank angle by looking out the side, then see what that bank angle looks like when you're looking out the front. Eventually you won't have to look out the side to know where your wingtip is. If you can't retain control of the airplane while checking the wingtip you probably shouldn't be practicing this maneuver yet.

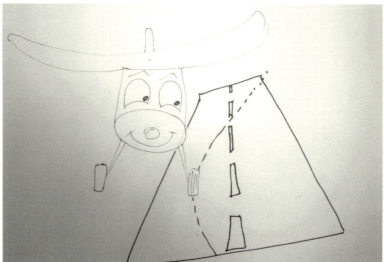

A happy airplane is one whose tire is tracking on a tangent to the curving course being flown.

As soon as your left tire touches the center line, lower your right wheel and raise the left wing, beginning a turn to the right.

You'll make an arcing turn from the left side of the center line and back toward it. As soon as your right tire touches the centerline lower the left, raise the right and repeat the process. Use the whole width of the runway. One of the keys to a graceful slalom is to visualize the course ahead of you and anticipate the centerline crossings. If you keep the curves equal you'll find it easier to maintain the correct amount of power, aileron, rudder and elevator in order to run true without scrubbing tires. If your tires start squealing they're telling you that you're not running true. By looking down the course and visualizing the curves you'll be able to keep the airplane's heading constantly on a tangent to the course.

The circle below represents the airplane's course line

The top arrow represents the tire's heading. It's on a tangent to the course line.

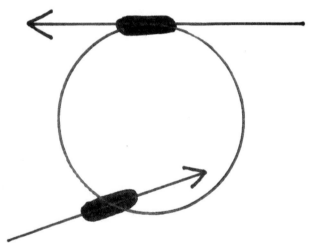

The bottom arrow represents the tire's heading if it is pointing inside the airplane's course. It's scrubbing from the outside in.

When up on wheel, the most common error is to use too much inside rudder. Remember: the purpose of rudder in this flight regime is NOT to compensate for adverse yaw. Instead it is to control the airplane's heading so that it is at a tangent to the curving course.

I often teach the slalom right after the landing in a turn because it's so easy to simply go from the initial landing turn to the next one in the opposite direction.

THE DUTCH TOUCH

Although simple in concept, the Dutch Touch is a maneuver I reserve for graduating final-phase students. I've practiced it a lot. I still find it difficult and often do it badly. In fact, I might even stop teaching it entirely! If you try it, you'll see why. In theory, it consists of a rapid series of Dutch Rolls performed so close to the ground that at the apex of each roll the tire on that side touches the ground.

It should not be attempted in a crosswind because of the possibility of scrubbing tires (Review the section on one-wheel work).

You'd think that the Dutch Touch would be a fairly easy maneuver. After all, you just take a simple maneuver like the Dutch Roll and perform it close to the runway. The problem is that, at altitude, we don't see the small altitude excursions the airplane makes as its lift vector changes. Because of that, I've found that the most common error is failure to coordinate elevator to compensate for changing amounts of lift as the aircraft's angle of bank changes.

And I'll confess that I've found this maneuver works best when I actually "plant" each wheel in its turn on the runway with a positive application of elevator. So much for thinking that it's the same as a Dutch Roll!

THE ONE-FOOTED TAKEOFF

The end of the runway is a great vantage point from which to observe the way people fly. It's the place we watch departing pilots in huge numbers drop their right wing shortly after liftoff because they don't know that it's rudder they should use to overcome left "turning" tendency. And speaking of rudder, that vantage point at the departure end of the runway is a great place to watch its misuse. Most tailwheel pilots will wag that rudder like crazy both on takeoff and landing. Watch them: That rudder will be fanning the air constantly as the pilot works at keeping the plane straight. Whether they know it or not, they are all working to gain an average angular deflection of the rudder that will give them the desired result. They simply travel to both sides of that sweet spot while it evades them. Now, don't think for a moment that I hold myself apart from this great gaggle of rudder-waggers. No, I'm as guilty as the next guy. But I do place great faith in practice. That's why I've set out to see if I can't reduce my tail-wagging to a minimum. Here's one way I'm working to achieve that elusive perfect rudder angle, at least during takeoff:

With wind on the nose, I line my plane up on the runway. I place my left foot on the floor (although poised for a desperate jump to the rudder pedal) and my right foot very lightly on the right rudder pedal. Then I advance the power. I know that the effects of "P" Factor and rotating prop wash, along with gyroscopic precession are going to try to cause my plane to yaw to the left. I will overcome that yaw with my right foot. But because my left foot is on the floor I'm going to be very careful not to over-rudder with my right foot and that is the key to this maneuver. Done properly, I can keep the plane on the centerline as it accelerates, through the tail coming up and through lift-off. I have to be especially careful as the tail rises. The prop disc is changing its angle relative to the direction of motion and several forces, including changing "P" Factor and gyroscopic phenomena are changing the amount of rudder that's necessary.

I can't always pull this one off. Sometimes I'm forced to hop onto the rudder pedal with that left foot because I used a bit too much right rudder and there aren't enough other forces to bring the nose back to the left. But I find that the more I practice it, the better I get and one thing I do know: I've decreased that amateurish rudder wagging down to a far more acceptable level. By keeping that left foot on the floor, I'm forcing myself to use restraint in the use of the right foot. See George DeMartini's "the flaring ratchet" in the "three-point landing" section. Developing restraint is often a good thing when we strive to perfect our techniques. Maybe I'll try this technique on landings next. Maybe not.

THE 360 DEGREE OVERHEAD APPROACH

I am consistently impressed by this simple fact: Most pilots cannot land power-off on a spot that is located 1,200 feet directly below them. If asked to land on that spot with a simulated engine failure, they will consistently overshoot it. They overshoot it because most pilots rush their turns in a power-off accuracy approach. They also arrive at short final going like a bat out of Hell. This high airspeed virtually guarantees that they will float forever and overshoot this basic accuracy landing. Why do they make these silly mistakes? Primarily because they will try to make one circle to the landing when they actually have plenty of room to make two or even three circles! This is a maneuver that merits a lot of practice. Y'know how everybody goes to "best glide" (or "best L/D") when confronted with an engine failure? Well, that speed will get you the farthest, but why go to a speed that gets you the farthest when the point to which you are flying lies directly beneath you? Wouldn't a slower speed that keeps you aloft longer (glider pilots call this "minimum sink") be a more prudent choice? Just something to think about.

In the last couple of years I've begun to really concentrate on a troika of maneuvers which will precede the Dead Stick Landing. The first two are the Minimum Altitude Loss Power-Off Turn and the 360 Degree Circling Overhead Approach. The third one is the Landing in a Turn.

Remember those pilots who couldn't land on a target 1,200 feet below them? Don't you be one of them. Their biggest problem was that they made only one circle because they didn't know how much altitude they would lose in a 360 degree turn. Let's not only learn how much altitude we lose in that turn, but also how to make such a turn with as little altitude loss as possible.

Through experimentation we'll learn that there are really only two parameters to pay attention to in this minimum altitude loss turn: Airspeed and bank angle. The first one is easy. Fly at Minimum Sink. "Duh". The second one is a bit harder. You'll be faced with the choice of steep or shallow bank. If you bank shallowly, you'll give up less of the vertical component of lift, but you'll take longer to complete your turn. If you bank steeply, you'll complete your turn in much less time, but you'll be giving up much more of the vertical component of your lift. With experimentation you'll find out that it's the steep bank which will lose the least amount of altitude. Somewhere between 45 and 65 degrees of bank will work just fine. You'll be on the verge of a stall and you must be perfectly coordinated. Just for an example, let's say that we discovered that this steeply banked, slow-speed turn resulted in a loss of 500 feet in 360 degrees of turn. That means we could be abeam the point of intended landing only 250 feet above the ground and still make it. That's why those guys screwed it up. They thought they had to be MUCH higher. So let's put what we've learned to use.

We circle right over the runway on which we intend to land. Each circle has one segment that is right over the runway on an upwind leg. That's another area most pilots get wrong. They'll circle with the center of their circle right over the center of the airport. When it comes time to make that last circle they'll be out of position. The diagram below shows the proper position of the circle.

Theoretically, the circles we fly could resemble a funnel like the one in which we drop coins and watch them spiral down to the bottom. That's because the angle at which we can glide will remain the same. So the higher we are the further away from the runway we can be. As we descend in a similar spiral, each circle would get smaller as we maintained the angle to the point of intended touchdown. That's an important thing to know but, in reality, I teach this technique with similar sized circles. Even the first circle, high above the airport, is roughly the same size as the last one down at about five hundred feet above the field. I do that so that we get more circles and thus more and better practice at the technique. It's that last circle where awareness of the glide angle will become important.

In the currently accepted method of flight instruction every student is taught to fly his pattern at "pattern altitude". Every airport has its published pattern altitude, usually 800 to 1,000 feet above the surface. That student is also taught to fly his downwind leg a certain distance away from the runway. They are almost never taught to fly at the resulting angle from the runway. My point is that the angle never changes, regardless of altitude. The only factors that change the angle are the glide ratio of the airplane you are flying and the wind. If you are lower but maintain the angle, you will fly closer and your turn from downwind to final will have to be tighter. The lower you are, the

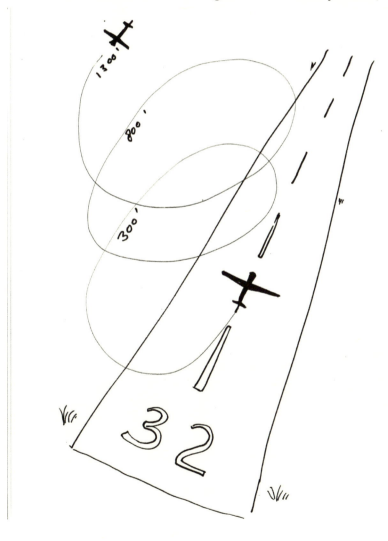

tighter that turn will have to be. If we are spiraling down to the runway, maintaining that angle, it will be obvious to us when we should make the last turn to a landing. There are several reasons I like this approach, but there is one that stands out and makes it well worth mastering: If you are cruising along cross country, have an engine failure and spot a nice, but relatively short spot in which to land, how would you know what the pattern altitude is for that nice little spot? You don't know what the field elevation is. Flying circles and angles will be the foolproof method to glide to a safe, accurate landing in that field. Everyone who has flown with me or read my articles knows how fond I am of that metaphor of the chicken coming home to roost. Well, here's the chicken who is so important to the practice of the circling approach: Everyone who has taken my Master Class or Tailwheel Endorsement course is familiar with minimum altitude loss turn and the circling approach. If they take the knowledge learned from that maneuver and apply it to the last turn of the circling approach, they realize that they can be a lot lower than they thought as they pass through the downwind leg. This knowledge and the skill that comes from practice can really save their bacon in the event of an engine failure followed by a power-off accuracy approach to a landing spot of an unknown altitude.

If you practice this approach and use the technique of constantly asking, "Am I high or am I low?" you'll soon get proficient. But you'll never get proficient if you don't practice it!

I have to admit that power-off accuracy approaches are the pilot operations on which I probably do the worst. That's why practice of these approaches is so important to me and may be to you as well.

THE GO-AROUND

Experts who study aviation accident statistics claim that go-arounds gone wrong account for a large percentage of flying accidents. They further claim that this fact points out that more training needs to be done in go-arounds.

I'll catch a bunch of flack for this statement, but here goes: I think the go-around is one of the most over-taught operations in modern flight training.

So why are pilots bending airplanes trying to accomplish an over-taught maneuver? I have a theory: Their ability to master fundamentals is so minimal that practice of the go-around is not the answer; mastery of fundamentals and simply changing from one gait (normal glide) to another (normal climb) is too much for them. Complex airplanes add to the complexity of the go-around but the fundamentals remain and should be mastered.

The decision making process is just as important as the skill to fly the go-around. I once watched a pilot die because he attempted a go-around when he should have just closed the throttles, slammed on the brakes and hoped for the best. We've created a mindset among modern pilots of "when in doubt, go-around". Certainly there is a time to go-around, but often the go-around is an over-reaction. A chimp can execute a go-around, but in the SRMC we teach the avoidance of obstacles on the runway during the landing, relying on greater piloting skill to avoid collision with objects, real or imagined. In the back of my mind is the possibility that someday I'll be approaching to land with a dead engine. Going around will not be an option. In such a circumstance I'd rather be riding with a SRMC graduate than some airplane herder whose only answer to sudden runway obstruction or a less than perfect approach is "go-around!"

Perhaps while flying with me, you'll learn to fly over tractors and deer on the runway or (my favorite) simply to raise one-wheel in order to avoid running over a turtle. Training maneuvers such as the slalom and multiple landings will further ensure that obstacle avoidance on landing or takeoff will simply not be a big deal to you in the future. And because a dead stick landing is always a possibility, I think pilots need to prepare to be committed to a landing when a go-around is not an option.

"DON'T MAKE STEEP TURNS CLOSE TO THE GROUND!"

Okay, here come the villagers with their torches and pitchforks, 'cause they're not gonna like this one at all!

Because modern pilots are taught to minimum standards, it must be assumed that their stick and rudder, seat-of-the-pants skills are minimal. What other reason could there be that students are cautioned never to try a turn back to the field (the "impossible turn") in case of engine failure and never to make tight (steep) turns close to the ground?

Students become high-time pilots who still carry those cautions echoing around in their heads. I guess it's assumed that the average pilot doesn't know how much altitude he loses in a power-off descending turn (see "The 360 Degree Overhead Approach") and that if he tightens up a turn, he's unable to recognize an imminent stall. Hmm, I wonder if most of their instructors would, either.

The truth is that in a power-off emergency landing, a tight turn close to the ground could spell the difference between life and death. Given the choice, my money is on the guy who's been trained well enough to be able to crank it around, then slip into a tight area and roll to a stop unhurt rather than the poor schmuck who can only follow some rule designed to protect the undertrained.

One of the reasons that instructors are so scared of steep turns is the fact that a 60 degree banked turn while maintaining altitude will result in 2 "G"s and increase by 40 percent the speed at which the aircraft will reach stalling angle of attack. Students have been taught to associate speed and bank angle with stall. They are rarely taught about acceleration or "G" force. Training airplanes are rarely equipped with "G" meters. Here's a little nugget of information: Angle of bank does not increase stall speed. "G" force increases stall speed (see "The Accelerometer" section of this book). Jim Dulin, in his excellent, but controversial, book, "Contact Flying", describes the technique of rolling into a steep bank and relaxing the back pressure until the turn is completed, then rolling out of the turn and increasing the back pressure to stop the altitude loss. I think this technique advocates what could be an important reflex to develop: When banking steeply close to the ground, think about "G" force and relax that back pressure to avoid the "G"-induced stall. And here's another important factor: If you can't roll into a steep bank without your nose dropping, you better practice. The pilot who has to pick his nose up because it dropped in that steep bank is the guy who's pulling more "G"s than the guy who never dropped the nose in the first place.

We're all scared to death of the classic stall spin on final. We tend to forget that the average aircraft will not spin if in a state of perfect coordination. That's why I get so concerned when my students skid the turn to final.

A fear of steep turns close to the ground can result in the classic scenario of the guy who's going to overshoot the turn from base to final. He's been taught not to bank steeply close to the ground but he knows he's gotta tighten the turn so he unconsciously mashes the rudder (Don't say "Oh, not me!" I remember doing it myself long ago). The resulting skid steepens the descent by pulling the nose down so he's forced to apply back pressure (he thinks) in order to both stretch the glide and get the nose up. The result is a half-turn spin into the ground. Guess he should have made a coordinated steep turn. Even with his wingtip inches from the ground he'd have been better off, wouldn't he?

FLAPS, POWER AND A WORD ABOUT ACCURACY

I teach that virtually every landing approach is power-off. Most flight schools teach a gradual power reduction approach, as well as a gradual flap application. Surprise! I'm against both of them and I'll explain why:

You may happily go through your entire flying career without ever experiencing an engine failure. But if you never practice for it, you'll probably fail that power-off-accuracy-approach drill miserably. Why not make most approaches power-off? It certainly won't hurt anything (you'll do a very gradual power reduction during the descent, so shock cooling isn't an issue) and you'll gain valuable practice against the possibility of the real thing.

Now, what about this gradual flap application thing? The main reason that gradual flap application is taught is the same reason every other stupid technique is taught: It's easier and doesn't require extra skill gained through practice. Modern flight instruction techniques were, for the most part, pioneered by aircraft manufacturers who realized that the easier they made learning to fly, the more pilots would be created and the more airplanes would be sold. Where do you think the nosewheel came from?

Why do we use flaps? Two reasons: Steeper approach (over an obstacle) without increasing airspeed and slower touchdown because of decreased stall speed, resulting in less tire wear and shorter landing.

Okay, since the steep approach is only required on final, why not wait for flap extension until we're actually ON final? Same for the second reason. If the flaps slow the landing then we don't need them until we're LANDING. Since flaps increase drag and shorten glide, it could be very likely that early, gradual flap extension will require the use of power to continue to the point of intended touchdown. If you lose an engine with flaps extended, you might not make it. Well, you do what you want to regarding the use of flaps, but if you're flying with me I won't allow them to be extended until the runway is assured and usually only on final. I might also ask that the flaps be retracted on final in order to extend the glide. Holy Cow! What heresy! That's a practice which is frowned upon because of the attendant loss of lift. However, a little experimentation will soon prove under what circumstances flap retraction in a glide is a good option. My thanks to Jerry Groendyke, one of the smartest fliers I know, for helping to organize my rationale on flap usage. You can send your hate mail to him and he can forward it to me.

THE SHORT FIELD LANDING

I have mildly criticized one of my primary students because she would initiate a three-point landing, touch down and then push the control wheel to raise the tail. I wanted her to keep that elevator back in order to demonstrate a "proper" three-point landing. She may not have been doing the landing by the book, but by raising the tail right after touchdown, she was getting the better of two techniques and I think we should all put this operation in our techniques toolbox. She would make a three-point landing, thus touching down at as slow a speed as possible. Then she'd push, transferring the weight of the plane onto its main gear and making its brakes as effective as they could be while she pounced on them. Needless to say, her elevator work was precise. She may have been one of the best students I've ever had. You can't make a shorter landing using any other technique (assuming you want to be able to use the airplane again!.

Use of brakes in a short field landing is an operation that scares many pilots. They are rightfully concerned about putting the aircraft on its nose. As a teacher I share their concern and get on my toes when teaching this technique. But I think it's important and I believe I may teach it more than I have in the past. Just remember that the risk of contacting the ground with the prop is very real when airspeed decreases. The precise use of elevator and brakes to prevent that event is very important. Be very careful about practicing this one! Any instructor must be on his toes, knowing that the brake is virtually the only control which he cannot override.

I fly with a lot of people who have little or no tailwheel time. What do many of these pilots have in common? Most are very concerned lest they smack that propeller on the runway.

Their fear originates with the realization that there is no nosewheel to prevent the prop from contacting the ground. So when I encourage them to raise the tail with full forward elevator on takeoff, many of them just don't believe me. They don't believe that they can be free with forward elevator and run no risk of prop smacking.

I have smacked a prop. I did it in front of thousands of air show fans at the Reno Air Races. When it comes to prop-smacking, I am the voice of experience. Believe me, it was a situation that none of you will ever experience unless you intentionally run your plane into a big cardboard box full of ducks. You can see my prop-smack on www.tailwheelersjournal.com. It's called "Reno Prop-Strike".

In a previous life I collided with a box of live ducks every summer weekend as an air show comedy pilot.

You are probably concerned that you can prop-smack the runway by lifting up the tail too far on takeoff. Let me tell you something: It ain't gonna happen. Let's go back to fundamentals to see why: The horizontal stabilizer is actually an upside down wing. Normally, its job is to push the tail down more as the airspeed increases. In this way, depending on the trim, the horizontal stabilizer and elevator control airspeed through a dynamic process called the Phugoid Oscillation (I love that name!). On takeoff, we ask the elevator and horizontal stabilizer to reverse their normal roles and raise the tail. That's pretty easy. After all, in a tailwheel airplane, the horizontal stabilizer is angled to do just that when the tail is on the ground. So we place the control wheel or stick fully forward as the plane accelerates. As the tail comes up, the horizontal stabilizer becomes level with the direction of flight.

If it rotates any further it incurs air loads that push it down. The more we accelerate, the harder the horizontal is pushed down and the more pressure it takes for us to try to make it come up past level. In fact, with full power and full forward stick it's almost impossible to raise the tail enough to contact the ground with the prop.

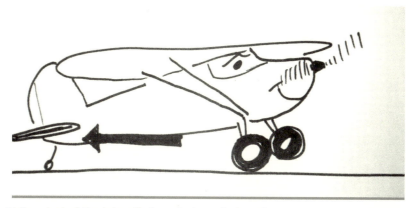

At the start of the takeoff, the relative wind pushes on the bottom of the horizontal stabilizer.

The slightest relaxation of forward pressure will keep the tail from going up any further. And that is why you don't have to worry about smacking the prop on takeoff. The reason I try to get my students to keep that tail up is so that the plane won't go "skippity-hop" off the ground as the weight gradually changes from the wheels to the wings. And that's what started this whole discussion.

On landing and subsequent deceleration, you can smack the hell out of it if you are not careful, so let's deal with that situation.

If you watch some air show performers, you'll see that they will sometimes taxi up to show center with the tail in the air, then bow to the crowd. The airplane is stopped, it's obviously developing a lot of power and the tail comes up causing the prop to move to within inches of the ground. This maneuver uses three controls to change the pitch of the airplane. Lots of power is used, depending on the wind force and direction. The brake is used, either dragging while taxiing tail-up or locked if the plane is stopped and bowing. Elevator is critical and its use must be very precise. Screw up one of those inputs or fail to compensate with another and the prop may become a backhoe.

As the tail comes up, the relative wind shifts to the top of the horizontal, making it difficult for the tail to come up further.

The technique above may not be one that you'll practice, but a variation of it is what a well-trained pilot will use in a short field landing. And under those same circumstances, an under-trained pilot will fail to use the resources available to him to keep his prop out of the dirt.

When an airplane is decelerating we've got the throttle closed. That leaves brake and elevator. I think either of them can be the culprit if the nose gets too low.

I've watched a couple of videos on YouTube that show props getting smacked. In the majority of them, it appeared to me that elevator was not used to maintain pitch. I hate to second guess other pilots, but that's what it looked like to me.

I consider elevator the primary pitch control in a braking, decelerating stop with the tail in the air. But as your airspeed decreases, your elevator will become less effective. And if you run out of elevator your braking will cause the plane to pitch down, so you've GOT to get off the brakes.

If you fail to control pitch with either brake or elevator, it's probably because you weren't aware of your precise pitch. That's usually caused by lack of proper concentration and not looking far enough away. It's **attitude flying** and that's what we're all about, isn't it?

I consider mastery of tail-up taxiing or quick stopping to be the sign of a well-qualified pilot. Like many operations it takes practice. The Whuffos at my former airport always assumed I was showing off with this maneuver. Whuffos don't understand the difference between showing off and practicing. That's what makes them Whuffos. I will also admit that I don't teach the technique very often. I can protect my students through most maneuvers by over riding their control inputs. One thing I can't do, though, is reduce their brake input. If they mash that brake and I run out of elevator we're going to have some bent tips. That's why I have to admit that I usually urge practice of this technique in someone else's airplane.

FLIGHT IN FORMATION

I suppose that most pilots will go through a lifetime of flying without ever attempting to share the same relatively small block of airspace with another airplane. For others, the ability to fly in close proximity with another airplane will be an important part of their flying skill set. In my opinion, every Commercial Pilot should be able to fly formation.

But sometimes the thrill of flying along up close to one of your buddies and the satisfaction of doing it with precision is all we need to make it a worthwhile experience. Throughout this little book, haven't I implied that increased skill is its own reward?

With George DeMartini flying, Janaé Smith prepares to shoot air-to-air of the Big Yellow Glider from the Cessna 140. George is the high time veteran, but both are formation pilots. Without formation flying skills, such a mission is impossible.

I don't presume to offer a complete formation flying treatise here. I will, however, give you a few little nuggets that have served me well. There are groups who have done an outstanding job of formalizing training in formation flying. Many are warbird groups who perform at airshows. A group of RV pilots are also doing a great job of teaching formation flying and organizing flights. I highly recommend utilizing the information that these groups have catalogued. Start by checking out www.vansairforce.com. I have immense respect for what these folks are doing for the practice of formation flying.

Like many pilot operations, formation flying is not easy at first. It has an element of danger. It is best learned in a formalized program but, like aerobatics, you're likely to learn it without such a program. So maybe we should look at some formation fundamentals that will help keep us safe, not only while we're learning, but also as we practice this valuable and satisfying skill.

Lead and Wing

For the purposes of this discussion we'll assume that our formation flights will consist of just two airplanes. One is the leader and one is the wingman. There can be no time that these roles are not clearly understood by both pilots. They may change their roles in mid-flight but each pilot must know which role he is playing. Just as many pilots and instructors insist on a verbal exchange to confirm who's flying the aircraft, a verbal affirmation of who is wing and who is lead is always appropriate. E.g., "I'm falling back now. You are lead".

"Roger, I am lead".

You absolutely cannot have a formation flight without a clear agreement on wing and lead.

Position relative to lead: Do I climb, descend or stay level in a turn?

In position, straight and level

Many pilots new to formation flying are confused about the wingman's position as the formation enters a turn. Do I stay at

111

the same altitude as the leader and assume his angle of bank in order to enter and complete the turn or do I maintain my position relative to the leader's airplane?

Maintaining our position in the turn.

That would mean that if I am on the left and the leader makes a right turn, I will climb and accelerate in order to maintain my position. If I am on the left and the leader makes a left turn, I will descend and decelerate in order to maintain my position. The correct technique is to climb or descend, to accelerate or decelerate in order to maintain your position RELATIVE to the leader's airplane We often use parts of his airplane lined up in order to maintain our position. For example, I'm putting the intersection of the lift and jury struts right over the center of the window.

Oops! Better climb when she turns!

You Gotta Be Able to Go Faster Than the Leader

In order to join with the leader and make necessary speed changes to stay in formation, the wingman must be able to accelerate and fly faster than the leader. If that's not possible, they should both stay on the ground and re-think this mission. With two airplanes of identical performance, the easiest way to accomplish this configuration is for the leader to simply use a lower maximum power setting. In dissimilar airplanes the same technique can be used or the slower airplane can fly lead. The wingman can also ask the leader to change power settings from time to time.

Just as it's necessary for the wingman to go faster than the lead, he must be able to slow down in order to join. This may be one of the most difficult parts of formation flying, but it's a fun challenge. In order to join up with the leader, the wingman must be able to catch the other plane, either by flying an interception course in a turn or simply going faster. In either case, once the leader is closed upon, the wingman will be faced with the need to slow in order to slide into and maintain his position. He must learn how his airplane decelerates and how to make it slow more quickly through the use of flaps, spoilers, forward slips and power reductions.

Love Them Gliders!

One of the best examples of formation flying technique can be seen in a motion picture my brother and I filmed many years ago. "Dawn Flight" is a live action short subject that features some intense formation flying scenes using Schweizer 1-26 sailplanes (You can get a DVD of this film at The Tailwheeler's Mercantile, on-line at www.tailwheelersjournal.com). Three gliders were used, two "story planes" in trail formation, followed by the "camera plane". You can see that the leader maintains about 25 percent spoilers throughout the flight. That gives the second ship the ability to close his spoilers and catch the leader. You can see him opening and closing his spoilers in order to maintain his position. The camera plane was flown by George Bernstein, the most experienced of the three pilots. His camera was attached to the nose of his glider and pointed forward. His job was not only to maintain his position at the back of the pack, but also to maintain the composition of his camera's shot.

Gliders are just about the best formation flying ships there are because of the tremendous control their spoilers afford them. They also lack propellers with which to do damage to each other. Even without an engine, they are much easier with which to fly formation. When I first flew the Big Yellow 2-32 glider in formation with a Cessna camera ship, I was absolutely blown away at how easy it was too swoop in to position with the camera plane and then simply open the spoilers and pitch up a bit in order to park it right there next to him. I was downright giddy when I discovered that!

How to Catch the Leader at First

When we first set out to practice formation flying, we must perform a joinup. If the wingman has the leader in sight, even a mile away, he can, with any excess speed, catch the leader. Depending on the amount of excess speed the wingman has, this can take a while! That's okay; we shouldn't be in a hurry. I think it's just fine to take time and learn how the planes accelerate and decelerate in a re-joining situation.

More Advanced Rejoins

Once we've re-joined a few times and practiced a few turns, climbs and descents, it's time for more advanced (and efficient) re-joins. I have to thank the late T.J. Brown for taking the time to give me dual instruction in this maneuver. T.J. flew his wife's Citabria while I flew my 100 HP J3 Cub. T.J would fly a circle and have me cut across that course in order to head him off. Not only did he instruct me in that method, but the former Air Force fighter pilot taught me how to use "G" force to create drag. He had me dive across the circular course. Because of the dive, my speed was far greater than his. But I was also below him so as I climbed up to position, the upward climbing of my plane created "G" force whose drag enabled me to swoop into my position. It's a complex maneuver and, depending on your natural ability can take some practice.   It took me a lot of practice.   I'm still practicing. But I do love swooping.

Types of Formations

There are different types of formations and they exist for different reasons. All must be mastered. The most common is Echelon. The wingman is to one side and slightly behind the leader. Line abreast finds the wingman directly to one side of the leader. Trail formation finds the wingman directly behind the leader, although he may be slightly below as well, the better to avoid the leader's propwash. When we fly gliders, we practice boxing the towplane's propwash. We descend down through it and explore its lateral limits. Such a drill may be helpful to formation fliers as well.

Remember when we stated that photography was one of the reasons we might need to fly formation? For the same reason, I've often found it was necessary to fly wing from in front of the leader. It's an awkward formation, but occasionally necessary, depending on the needs of the photo mission.

Who's Looking at Whom?

In one of my favorite cartoons, Mickey, Donald and Goofy are on vacation. They are driving their cartoon car pulling their cartoon travel trailer on a mountain road with lots of bends. As the car and trailer round a curve, the axles stretch as the "G" force pulls the trailer toward the outside of the turn. Cartoonists understand "G" force better than many pilots!

The three travelers sit down to lunch at their little dinette in the trailer. Out the window we can see the countryside whizzing past. Mickey looks around at the group and suddenly has a thought.

"Hey, who's driving?" he asks.

"Huh hyuk! I am!" declares Goofy.

Just as Goofy couldn't possibly be driving AND enjoying lunch in the trailer with his buddies, you can't be the leader while staring at the wingman and making corrections to the formation.

When I was training a young tow pilot in the art of formation flying, I noticed that he was spending a lot of time watching me when he was lead.

"Don't look at me, Poophead!" I admonished him. It became an oft-quoted line in our little crew. The leader needs to be watching where the flight is going, concentrating on his own maintenance of altitude and heading as well as traffic and terrain. The wingman is concentrating on the leader. That's as it should be. Unfortunately that's also why entire formation teams have impacted terrain together. The wingmen were doing their job. You may want to ask yourself, "Do I trust my leader?"

He may want to ask, "Do I trust my wingman?"

The advanced formation practice of landings and takeoffs puts a greater responsibility on the leader. He's truly flying for two and must make room for his wingman when on or close to the ground.

The first time I did many formation takeoffs and landings was while flying across Texas in two 450 Stearman biplanes with Earl Cherry. It was a real kick in the pants (and also my first experience with GPS. ("Hey, Earl, I think my wingtip is in Mexico!"). It certainly tests a wingman's concentration when it comes time to land.

I'd suggest that you don't even think about landing and taking off in formation until you've mastered the fundamentals of rejoins and basic maneuvering at altitude.

Know Your Limitations

Although an accomplished formation pilot should be able to fly close, don't ever let yourself be pressured to fly closer than a distance with which you are comfortable. As Clint Eastwood said, "a man's gotta know his limitations". Know yours.

Needing a perch for a cameraman, I once asked a pilot if she could fly formation. She said she could. Being a trusting sort, I loaded the photographer aboard her 182 and off we went to get some shots. I only saw her again a couple of times and she was about a mile away. It was a total waste of time. Obviously, her idea of formation flying and mine were a little different. I don't think she knew her limitations! Be honest with yourself and others regarding your abilities. There are pilots with thousands of hours of flight time who can't fly formation. There are some with a couple of hundred hours who can do a good job of it. The difference is knowledge, practice and opportunity.

While still a student pilot, Janaé Smith slides into Line Abreast formation with my Big Yellow Glider.

When Do I Bail?

Perhaps the most important consideration in formation flying is that we mustn't trade paint with the other guy. That's why the wingman must exit the formation immediately if he loses sight of the leader. There is normally a direction that will satisfy the need for safe egress. If the leader was on your left when you lost sight of him, it's probably safe to assume that you can exit safely to the right. You may be in a climbing, descending or level turn, depending on the circumstances. Hold that exit heading for a while and communicate with the leader. Someone's got to have a visual on the other before a rejoin can be attempted.

Some Common Sense Rules

The leader must know he is the leader. The wingman must know he is the wingman. I know it sounds silly, but it needs to be stated.

All pilots in a formation must clearly agree on who is "wing" and who is "lead" at all times. Lead changes may be made in flight, but there must be no time when those roles are at all ambiguous. This is perhaps the one item that is most misunderstood by the neophyte.

The leader does not have to be able to see the wingman at all times but the wingman must always have the leader in sight. If the wingman loses sight of the leader, he must exit the formation in a predetermined safe direction. A re-join can be attempted once safe separation is accomplished and one participant has the other in sight.

Communication is important. No formation flight should be attempted or continued without clear communications on a predetermined and suitable radio frequency.

While there is a place for "throw-together" formation flights, normally they should be briefed ahead of time.

Maybe We'll Get Serious About This!

At "The Tailwheeler's Journal" we do a lot of tailwheel endorsements. We may start getting serious about formation flying. Obviously, it's an increase in complexity, expense and personnel for us. If you'd like to participate in a Formation Flying Course, let us know. We may start putting one together. For me, it will be an extension of what I normally do... I've always stated that there are two roles for the Flight Instructor: To teach and to protect. I must impart the skills to perform the operations that I teach and I must protect you while you are learning those skills. I see no reason why we can't include formation flying in the collection of skills we teach.

A PARTING WORD

When I started writing this little book YouTube and Vimeo had not been invented. Lately I've found them to be a fount of knowledge. Looking at examples of prop strikes was a huge educational experience for me, as has study of piloting techniques at the Valdez, Alaska Bush Pilots' Fly-In. I highly recommend it.

How appropriate that we end this project with the subjects of practice, flight training and safety. I have been told that I'm a pretty good stick. That's very nice. Everyone likes praise. But if you have natural talent, how can you accept praise for something that's in your genes? The reason I take pride in my abilities is precisely because I am not a natural flying talent. Everything I do well I do well because I practiced it long and hard. Bob Hoover, one of the greatest pilots I've ever known, points out that he doesn't believe his abilities are special. Rather, he points out that he has had opportunities and has chosen to practice. Modern flight instruction has labored to keep pilots from getting close to "the envelope". Personally, I think we're capable of getting a rough idea of where the edge of the envelope is. We don't have to bump up against it. But I think we can use intelligent practice to gain skills which will enable us to fly far better than some of our teachers ever thought we could and to explore those areas of expertise which, although safely clear of the edge of the envelope, are still far beyond the abilities of those who are satisfied to perform to minimum standards.

In case you hadn't noticed it, I feel that modern flight instruction fails miserably in developing much skill in those who are taught in the vast majority of flight schools. Why is this? There are several reasons.

For one thing, in aviation we have this unique situation where teaching is the job which new pilots can slide right into in order to build time and eventually land that airline job they've been lusting after. That leaves those who are just entering our little flying world to learn from those who know the least
.

Modern flight schools are also consumed with safety. That's pretty understandable and, in many cases, commendable. A desire to be safe often causes the pursuit of the most conservative actions. Unfortunately, the practice of conservative operations often deprives the student of the opportunity to learn to fly skillfully. The long, straight-out departure is just one such example.

Civilian flight training, as a rule, doesn't "wash out" any students. Compare that with the military, where a large percentage of those who pursue flight training are judged not good enough and are washed out to pursue another activity. I've long been a fan of military training and that's one reason.

If we want to produce safe pilots, we'd better train pilots who have a much higher skill level than is currently found in the majority of pilots. We can do that by upping the difficulty level of those operations and maneuvers we teach. But in order to do that safely, we must provide those student pilots with teachers who have the ability to keep them safe as they practice those maneuvers. As Hamlet said, "Aye, there's the rub!"

I can teach my students to execute a landing in a turn which will save their butts if they're called upon to put a powerless airplane into a tiny little spot when there's no altitude remaining for that nice, long approach they were taught at the Acme Flying School. But I can only do that because I've taken the time to get reasonably competent at it myself. I've been teaching that maneuver since I had about two thousand hours, much of that time spent practicing exacting maneuvers and aerobatics. It's not me, it's the experience. Create a way to provide that experience to more pilots and you'll find a way to provide better instructors to those who want to learn to fly. Easy for me to say, huh? I doubt if it will ever happen.

Safety will always be the paramount goal of all of us who teach flying (except for a few schools where profits are actually paramount). Some will pursue safety by teaching low-time students to fly in a manner that will require less skill. Others of us will continue to increase safety by demanding a higher level of skill from those who fly with us. We will develop that skill by protecting those students while they practice operations and maneuvers which require a higher level of skill. Which method is better? I think mine is, but it sure isn't perfect!

Even if you don't agree with some of my more heretical theories, perhaps this little book has caused you to question some "conventional wisdom" and perhaps inspired you to simply go out and practice. I can't stress enough the importance of increasing your competence through the practice of more difficult pilot operations such as accuracy landings, one-wheel work, aerobatics and my favorite, formation flying.

Thanks for putting up with me and enjoy the gift of flight.

Happy Swooping!

Brian Lansburgh

About the Author

Brian Lansburgh is the founder of the Website, www.tailwheelersjournal.com. He is a working flight instructor, specializing in tailwheel endorsements.

An Academy Award nominated filmmaker and former Air Show pilot, Lansburgh writes regular articles for the Tailwheeler's Journal and produces videos for that website as well as for selected clients. His audio CD, "Nuts from a Blind Squirrel" features selected stories in a delightful audio book style.

Readers of Brian's Flying Book are encouraged to sign up to receive regular newsletters from the Tailwheeler's Journal. The Newsletters alert readers to new articles and videos as they are posted on the increasingly popular website.

Front and rear cover photographs are by Bert Garrison. Garrison works closely with Lansburgh on the Videography of the Tailwheeler's Journal and is an acclaimed still photographer. Much of his work can also be seen on his website, www.aerialpixel.com. Besides being a talented photographer and videographer, Garrison flew the U-2 and SR-71 "Blackbird" while an Air Force pilot. He is currently a captain for Southwest Airlines.